The Complete Handbook for

FAMILY LIFE MINISTRY

IN THE CHURCH

The Complete Handbook for FAMILY LIFE MINISTRY IN THE CHURCH

Don W. Hebbard, Ed.D.

OLIVER NELSON

THOMAS NELSON PUBLISHERS
Nashville • Atlanta • London • Vancouver

Published in Nashville, Tennessee, by Thomas Nelson, Inc., Publishers, and distributed in Canada by Word Communications, Ltd., Richmond, British Columbia.

The Bible version used in this publication is THE NEW KING JAMES VERSION. Copyright © 1979, 1980, 1982, Thomas Nelson, Inc., Publishers.

Library of Congress Cataloging-in-Publication Data

Hebbard, Don W., 1957–
    The complete handbook for family life ministry in the church / Don W. Hebbard.
        p.   cm.
    ISBN 0-7852-8191-6 (pbk.)
    1. Church work with families.   2. Church and education.   3. Christian education.   I. Title.
BV4438.H43   1995
255'.1—dc20   94-40462
                                                                                   CIP

Printed in the United States of America.
                1 2 3 4 5 6 — 00 99 98 97 96 95

To Dr. Royce Money
President, Abilene Christian University

Pioneer, Teacher, Mentor, and Friend

Contents

Foreword

Family Life Ministry—What do these words mean to you? Special programs, the newest fads, outside speakers, or a well-integrated ongoing ministry supported by the senior minister? We all have a choice of either ignoring the faltering families in our society or reaching out to them with the gospel and watching family lives change. That's what this book is all about.

Here at last is a practical step-by-step resource based upon years of experience as well as a sound educational and biblical base. This book will be useful for churches that are considering *developing* a family ministry as well as those seeking to strengthen or revamp an *already existing* program.

The author of this book believes that the foundation for a successful ministry begins with a period of serious prayer and study concerning family ministry. Also necessary is a critical examination of "who we are and what our mission is in this place." I agree! As you read through the table of contents you will catch both the vision and thoroughness of Dr. Don Hebbard. Step by step, he will then take you through the process of making a difference in the lives of family members in your church. This is a book we needed years ago, and I'm thankful it's finally here.

H. Norman Wright
Marriage, Family, Child Counselor
Director of Christian Marriage Enrichment

Acknowledgments

I wish to thank the supportive people at Thomas Nelson Publishers; Lila Empson, Esther Fitzpatrick, Marie Sennett, and Sharon Gilbert; for all their help. My special thanks to Victor Oliver whose dedication to this book made the project a reality.

Thanks to Jennifer, my loving wife, and her father, Col. Glen Johnson. Through the years you have been committed to me and to the dreams of family ministry. Your support during the down times always strengthened my soul.

I want to thank two very important congregations in my life: the North Atlanta Church of Christ and the South MacArthur Church of Christ. I appreciate the elders, ministers, and members for their love of family life ministry.

Finally I want to thank three very special friends; Scott Johnson, and Dwain and Sheri Brown; for their company, humor, and love.

Introduction

I have heard it said that behind every book is a story. In the fall of 1981, I was among six graduate students attending Dr. Royce Money's first course in family ministry at Abilene Christian University. We normally convened class in the local doughnut shop where Royce shared stories of his pioneering family life ministry in Springfield, Missouri. The direction of my ministry was changed forever by that one class.

Perhaps as a church leader you have struggled with anxiety over the condition of families in your church and community. What can the church do? I found an answer in family life ministry. Maybe you will too. Family ministry may be one of the most biblical and practical ministries any church can attempt. But it is not a catalog of programs. It is a way of thinking about ministry. It is a "new" philosophy of ministry that is as old as the Bible itself.

I hope as you read this book you will come to view it as a pioneers' map charting the territory ahead for you. Many sources exist that encourage the church to minister to families, but few tell us how to do it. I will raise questions, offer guidelines, and suggest models to help you construct your own unique family ministry in the context of your church setting. I pray this text will serve to stimulate your own creativity and initiative.

Finally, I hope you catch a dream for family life ministry in your church. We need church leaders and ministers with an intense passion for families. This envisioning will refuel your motivation for ministry. You may catch a vision of ministering like the Master. Your church will be blessed, hurting families will be blessed, and you will thank God that He has allowed you to serve families.

Prologue

Therefore, when the Lord knew that the Pharisees had heard that Jesus made and baptized more disciples than John (though Jesus Himself did not baptize, but His disciples), He left Judea and departed again to Galilee. But He needed to go through Samaria.

So He came to a city of Samaria which is called Sychar, near the plot of ground that Jacob gave to his son Joseph. Now Jacob's well was there. Jesus therefore, being wearied from His journey, sat thus by the well. It was about the sixth hour.

A woman of Samaria came to draw water. Jesus said to her, "Give Me a drink." For His disciples had gone away into the city to buy food.

Then the woman of Samaria said to Him, "How is it that You, being a Jew, ask a drink from me, a Samaritan woman?" For Jews have no dealings with Samaritans.

Jesus answered and said to her, "If you knew the gift of God, and who it is who says to you, 'Give Me a drink,' you would have asked Him, and He would have given you living water."

The woman said to Him, "Sir, You have nothing to draw with, and the well is deep. Where then do You get that living water? Are You greater than our father Jacob, who gave us the well, and drank from it himself, as well as his sons and his livestock?"

Jesus answered and said to her, "Whoever drinks of this water will thirst again, but whoever drinks of the water that I shall give him will never thirst. But the water that I shall give him will become in him a fountain of water springing up into everlasting life."

The woman said to Him, "Sir, give me this water, that I may not thirst, nor come here to draw."

Jesus said to her, "Go, call your husband, and come here."

The woman answered and said, "I have no husband."

Jesus said to her, "You have well said, 'I have no husband,' for you have had five husbands, and the one whom you now have is not your husband; in that you spoke truly."

The woman said to Him, "Sir, I perceive that You are a prophet. Our fathers worshiped on this mountain, and you Jews say that in Jerusalem is the place where one ought to worship."

Jesus said to her, "Woman, believe Me, the hour is coming when you will neither on this mountain, nor in Jerusalem, worship the Father. You worship what you do not know; we know what we worship, for salvation is of the Jews. But the hour is coming, and now is, when the true worshipers will worship the Father in spirit and truth; for the Father is seeking such to worship Him. God is Spirit, and those who worship Him must worship in spirit and truth."

The woman said to Him, "I know that Messiah is coming" (who is called Christ). "When He comes, He will tell us all things."

Jesus said to her, "I who speak to you am He" (John 4:1–26).

The story of Jesus' conversation with the Samaritan woman outside the village of Sychar represents the model text for family life ministry. Jesus blessed the woman with the gifts of acceptance, hope, and healing.

This book is about family life ministry. In it we will discuss many of the practical steps a family life minister can take to help the local congregation address the needs of contemporary families in the church and the community.

But the real challenge of family ministry is presented by this wonderful story. It is a challenge to sit by wells. Before we can effectively minister to people, we must learn to sit by their wells and listen.

We must sit by the well at the day care center in the early morning hours. We must sit by the well in the emergency rooms. We must sit by the well and hear the cries of the young mother who lost an infant or the widow who buried her partner of fifty years.

Family ministry begins and ends with men and women who have learned to sit by wells. Family ministry is not a collection of programs. It is an attitude of ministry, a way of thinking about and addressing the daily struggles of families. In the final analysis, its effectiveness will be determined by who we are as transparent costrugglers in relationship with the people we serve.

A ministry to families is something that some churches will do well and others will do poorly. But it is something that each congregation will do. Those who do it well will have learned to sit by wells.

The Complete Handbook for

FAMILY LIFE MINISTRY

IN THE CHURCH

1
LEARNING TO SIT BY WELLS

A dilapidated three-story house sits on Peachtree Street in downtown Atlanta. It is the birthplace of Margaret Mitchell. As I stood looking at her writing desk, I was reminded of the now famous railroad yard scene in *Gone with the Wind*.

The camera panned slowly to the left as Scarlett walked into literally acres of wounded Confederate soldiers. She was searching for Dr. Meade to come and deliver a baby, but she found herself lost in a sea of dying men from the battle of Atlanta. When she finally located the physician and made her request, he scolded her, "They're dying right before my eyes, and there is nothing I can do. Now run along home, child."

I am often asked what family life ministry is all about. Family life ministry is the railroad yard with families falling all around us. Calls come in to me daily from church leaders and ministers crying, "Our families are dying out here. What can we do?"

The purpose of this book is to be a practitioner's guide. It is intended for ministers or church leaders who want to roll up their sleeves and get to work in the fight for the American family. Those of us in the local church are in the ideal position to make a direct and immediate impact on the quality of family life in this country if we are willing to step on to the city streets.

The bad news is, there is a great deal of work to be done. Marriages and families are suffering tremendously. The good news is, with all that pain they are more open and receptive to God's plan for the family than ever before.

Jesus by the Well

Where do you begin if you want to build a family life ministry? How do you get started if you want to be a family life minister? I believe you begin by learning to sit by wells.

Jesus met a Samaritan woman at Jacob's well outside the city of Sychar. He visited first with her about a drink, but He ended the conversation talking about the living water from God. John records that "many of the Samaritans of that city believed in Him because of the word of the woman who testified" (John 4:39).

What did Jesus do that had such an impact on people's lives? He listened to them. But more than that, He crawled inside their skins and itched where they itched. He learned to sit by wells and understand the human condition. Then He could effectively speak to their suffering. Paul reflected this desire to sit with people by wells when he wrote, "But [Jesus] made Himself of no reputation, taking the form of a bondservant, and coming in the likeness of men. And being found in appearance as a man, He humbled Himself and became obedient to the point of death, even the death of the cross" (Phil. 2:7–8).

Counselors call this the power of empathetic listening. Jesus understood that if He spent time living with people and walking the walk, He could more effectively minister to them.

During the decade of the 1980s, the old Red County Courthouse was one of the busiest buildings in the downtown area of Dallas. Through its courts passed many men, women, and children who were victims of divorce.

If we asked those people what role the local church played in their lives, many would say, "None!" If we probed further, we would discover that many saw no relevance between what occurred on Sunday morning and what happened in their everyday lives. Am I laying the failure of the American family at the doorstep of the local church? Certainly not. Individuals must take personal responsibility for their decisions.

However, a great challenge exists to all church leaders to learn to sit by wells and take up the struggle for family life. Each semester I teach family ministry, I ask my students to spend several hours sitting by a community well. They spend time in emergency rooms, divorce courts, and halfway houses. The exercise is absolutely mandatory for any minister wishing to help families. Robbie Robinson tells her story of learning the meaning of well sitting and ministry at a truck stop:

I walked inside the truck stop along with "Why Not Me" and the Judds on the big screen television. Truckers were running around that place like kids on a playground—and it was a little after 8:00 A.M. Cups of coffee and cigarette smoke were cliches as I made myself comfortable in a booth, complete with telephone.

I sat for a while and was served by the waitress, all of the men having been waited on. She erased the flirtatious smile from her face as her eyes contacted mine. I was directed to the breakfast bar and was quickly abandoned. The booths were all filled, but with only one man each. Most of the men were sipping coffee slowly and simply "being." A few were attempting to catch up on the lives of their children and to carry on a peaceful conversation with their wives.

I made my way up to the heap of scrambled eggs, bacon, and pancakes. I noticed men coming out of the showers, somewhat renewed, but at least clean. On the other side of the store were rows and rows of magazines on which many women were present, substituting for others who could not be there. "The Best of . . ." cassettes lined the shelves along with T-shirts, caps, and a few Louis L'Amour westerns.

Probably eight men expressed concern for my welfare, seeing that I was alone. One fellow gave me five dollars "for a cup of coffee on me." I listened to him talk about the divorce he and his wife were working through. I just listened with a sympathetic ear to his struggle with custody suits and loneliness. Several fellows left the scene promptly after I informed them of my degree and career plans. A few did not. A few asked me about God. One even affirmed me.

I was at that truck stop for about three hours and didn't particularly want to leave. I feel I might have reminded a few of the fellows of someone far away—most of them I think could see their daughter in me. It hurt to see that look in their eyes. It was the kind of look that makes you hang your head and count your blessings. I couldn't help but pray for those men and women there who have never had the love and luck I've had, and who probably never will.

The truck stop also had an ironic warmth to it. Everybody there was in the same boat. Everyone was needing money, companionship, and a purpose. I hated the thought that most of their purposes were merely to bring home themselves and a monetary support on the weekends. I couldn't imagine a relationship by phone day in and day out. But it was a reality to those fellows.

I noticed that most seemed somewhat renewed. . . . In a trucker's usual two-hour stay, he would get gas, eat, relax, read, and socialize—refuel. Most did not seem to have meaningful relationships there, except with the waitresses, whom they would see periodically. They come in weary and bored and leave filled, but not whole.

I wondered as I ate if I could have handled such a career—could I be gone all week like that? Could I handle the loneliness? Suddenly

C.B.'s made lots of sense. It was their identity—their own language, their own inside jokes, their own special refuge. Suddenly the girls on the magazines did not seem so dirty. Both the girls and truckers needed the "companionship" so bad that the price never seemed too high for having a brief moment of wonderful contact, real or not.

It occurred to me that this truck stop was ironically similar to the church. Ministers serve others, feeding individual needs. Seeing the same ministers and members every week is meaningful and peace-bringing to members. Truckers take showers and feed their bodies. Worship cleanses hearts and feeds souls. Peace and rest are found from the 75-mile-per-hour world of deadlines and destinations.

However, this ideal is just that. If you are a "visitor," you are not necessarily treated with the level of respect given to those who are "regulars." Most sit alone, even if surrounded by others with the same circumstances. Sometimes hurting people are listened to. Most people mistake the pulpit for a big screen TV. People pay what they owe and leave.

Truckers taught me a lot about the difference between God's reality and human reality. Things holy and just are not found very often. Hurting people continue to hurt in our churches. They leave with the same pain they come in with. My job as a future minister has really little to do with impressing and perfection. It has more to do with those who come to refuel and "rest." Who will ever want to work overtime if he or she never feels *heard?* That is the guarantee God gives me, and it is the guarantee I must come with as a minister.

It is not my job to fix, but to listen, feed, and be an agent of peace and grace. My purpose is simple. I will be a waitress, a servant. My reward comes from the management and not often from the customer. I am here to please God, not men!

The family minister must feel the exhaustion of a mother at 6:00 A.M. dropping off her child at day care. Walk with an undercover drug unit into a drug bust. Admit a loved one into an inner-city hospital at 3:00 A.M. for an overdose. Stand in the grocery store checkout line at 5:45 P.M. with all the working mothers. Mourn with the young couple who lost their child from SIDS (sudden infant death syndrome). Sit in a divorce court as a husband and a wife carve up their possessions and their life together.

Family ministry is grief work. It is the ability to walk in the pain of the human predicament and the plan of the eternal Father. It continually draws the minister back to an awareness of the human lack of wisdom, the comfort of the Word of God, and the need for grace in all our lives. This is not glamorous ministry. This is not ministry in the spotlight of a major television network. But this is ministry that will cause whole households and villages to believe because they see the testimony of one fallen child of God touched by the healing hand of the Savior.

A Working Definition

Defining terms is dangerous business. Something always seems to be omitted. Nevertheless, for the purpose of organizing our thinking and approaching the building of family ministry in the local church, I suggest the following working definition: *Family life ministry is ministry of the church through preventive and therapeutic efforts designed to strengthen all forms of families in the church and the community.*

This definition embodies the five key questions that you must answer if you are to build a sound family life ministry. Let's look at the first question.

Is This Ministry?

What an elementary question! But it is one that church leaders and members often ask me. The local church must believe that a part of Christ's ministry in the world today includes helping all families grow stronger. This is the critical starting point for anyone considering an organized effort.

Some people are concerned about whether family life ministry is part of the biblical pattern of ministry. Did Jesus intend for His church to be involved in family issues? Jesus ministered to people's felt needs. If they were hungry, He fed them. If they were sick, He healed them. If they needed leadership, He led them. Even a casual survey of His sermon topics would evoke tremendous interest in any pulpit this week—gossip, adultery, stealing, work, and parenting, to name a few. Jesus ministered to the felt needs of people to demonstrate the love of God and direct humankind to the Father.

You must also look at the personality of the congregation. What kind of family ministry would suit your church and community? Family ministry in its full-developed form as described in this book may not be the best option for every church. The price tag is high, and the rewards are often intangible and difficult to measure quantitatively. The work is slow and filled with defeats and heartaches. But the rewards are spiritually solid for the church that commits itself to this ministry.

Where do you and your church begin? The foundation for a successful ministry begins with a period of serious prayer and study concerning family ministry, and a critical examination of who you are and what your mission is in this place. Once this step has been taken, you are ready to consider a second question.

Is the Focus to Be Prevention or Therapy?

What kind of help are you going to provide? Are you going to set up a counseling ministry offering group meetings? Are you going to offer programs and classes designed to head off problems before they get out of hand? Are you going to do both? Is there a priority, and if so, what is it? These are basic questions you must ask as you and your church hammer out a philosophy of family ministry.

How are you going to minister? What will be most effective in your situation? You cannot answer these questions in a vacuum. You must face them with information on the local church, available internal resources, other programs being offered, and current issues facing the community. Each local situation is unique.

I strongly believe there is a priority, and many churches are in an ideal position to capitalize on that priority. Families desperately need positive models. They need resources to handle their difficulties. They want encouragement that they are doing something right!

From a practical standpoint, how do you do this? Figure 1.1 illustrates where family life ministry can affect the developmental and situational crises in a person's life. Certain crises are a natural part of the developmental process. Marriage, the birth of a child, and midlife adjustments are examples of these crises; they are illustrated by the boxes. Unforeseen events such as sickness or the loss of a job can also affect someone negatively; these situational crises are represented by the circles.

Family ministry tries to prepare people for the developmental crises and assist them through the situational crises. Let's explore one example. In our church we offered a community enrichment class during the regular Wednesday night program. It was designed and operated expressly for community guests. Topics and speakers addressed needs we had identified through community needs analysis. Exciting things began to happen. The guests enjoyed having their own class. They didn't mind being new, and after a few visits, they made themselves right at home. Several came regularly for months.

We also discovered our members wanted to get involved. The curriculum was suited to their needs. Members and guests came together, bonded by a common struggle. The vital connection so many churches struggle to make between church and community was made naturally and effectively. The connecting point was the family.

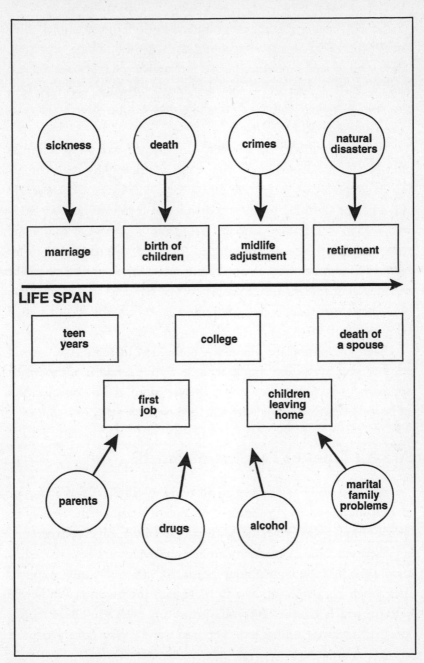

Fig. 1.1. Life crises

So am I saying that the church need not offer professional guidance? No, the two—prevention and therapy—cannot be separated. They tend to feed on each other. As preventive programs are offered, families surface with needs that demand counseling. The reverse is also true. As people call for counseling, they can be directed to educational programs of the church.

A tenderhearted man came to one of our parenting seminars after he saw an ad in the newspaper. He was struggling with parenting an adopted daughter while caring for a wife dying of cancer. He was a parent, husband, nurse, taxi driver, and owner of his own business—all in one fragile package. While the course gave him some parenting tips, the counseling helped him deal with the stress in his family. He later came to be one of the most active supporters of our ministry and brought many people to our seminars and events. The combination of therapy and prevention gave him the tools to cope with his situation.

Each church must decide what is the best fit for it. The second stage of your evaluation should include a consideration of the major approach to take (prevention and therapy mix) and a consideration of how prevention and therapy will feed on each other.

Are All Types of Families Included?

Are you ready to minister to all types of families? You and your church may need to expand the concept of what a family really is. Our communities are filled with single adults, divorced parents, single-parent families, blended families, and widows. I believe each is a valid family type with unique needs. An effective family ministry must reach out to people who don't fit into the traditional life cycle pattern, which assumes everyone grows up, goes to college, gets a job, gets married, and has kids. The past twenty years have produced more families we are only now coming to understand.

If ministers and Sunday school teachers implicitly say, "You are accepted at this church only if you are a traditional family with Mom at home and Dad out earning a living," we can expect to minister only to these families, and that is a tragic mistake.

The local church must be willing to minister to families of all forms. I believe the unwritten rules of exclusion are sinful and contrary to the teachings of Christ. I know of churches that would be double their size if they had kept the members they lost during a family crisis.

Defining the family in God's household has a profound impact on the philosophy of ministry and the way you carry out the tasks of day-to-day ministry. This step cannot be assumed. It must be taught and retaught.

Is the Target the Church or the Community?

Who will you and your church primarily minister to, local church folks or the community? This is the inreach versus outreach question. The answer will define the target for the ministry.

My first family ministry was targeted toward outreach. We aimed all our offerings at unchurched people in the community. An interesting residual effect occurred. As we offered programs to our neighbors, we stirred up excitement and met needs in our church family. We began with outreach but accomplished inreach. We found the issues facing our community were reflected in our church. When we helped our neighbors cope with this crisis, we also helped ourselves.

Effective inreach and outreach must begin with needs analysis. This is the systematic process of discovering existing needs in the church or community, identifying resources to meet those needs, and designing effective programs. Quality family ministry demands that you do your homework first.

The next step is to determine the target. If it is the church, you have plenty of work to do. If it is the community, you need to see the church through their eyes. Both efforts demand a comprehensive needs analysis.

Your decision-making process now includes determining the target of your efforts (church, community, or both) and identifying their needs (comprehensive needs analysis).

Can It Fit in Here?

The final question is one of integration. Can family ministry be integrated into the existing life of your church? If it can, you have the potential for a dynamic ministry.

To be effective, family ministry must work in concert with other existing ministries. It must be a commitment for the long haul to effect change among families.

A solid family ministry must have a strong relationship with the minister in the pulpit. Dr. Royce Money states, "Family ministry must be a continual pulpit theme that no Mother or Father's Day sermon can make up for." Family ministry integrates well with the education ministry of the church. Youth groups and young people's activities can be included naturally into the work. Young couples programs, nursery, senior citizens, and evangelism—all can interact with a flexible family ministry that adapts to the unique needs of each church (see fig. 1.2).

A dynamic family ministry can be the common denominator in a multiministry church to promote cooperation and interaction among ministries. So, your decision-making process expands to include these questions: How do we view ministry at our church? Would family life ministry fit in? What ministries would effectively integrate with this new emphasis? What ministries would be hesitant?

With current resources, any church large or small can minister in some degree to its families. Church leaders who are seriously considering a full-time commitment to this area need to plan clearly at each stage of development and take into account all the issues raised in this section. With these decisions firmly in mind the foundation for a family ministry can be laid.

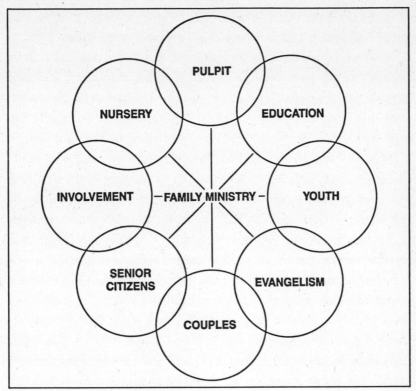

Fig. 1.2. Integration of ministries

A Call for Pioneers

When I was in the sixth grade, builders constructed a new house on the corner. The new neighbors were not yard people. The grass grew several feet high to the dismay of the whole neighborhood. I offered my services and began cutting one hot August day. The Texas sun scorched my back as I inched the mower ahead just enough to take about two feet of heavy grass under the blade. The mower choked and died during three days of work. When I finished, the new neighbors paid me five dollars and warned me next time to do a better job of cleaning off the sidewalk when I was through! Cutting down that jungle cost a great deal and resulted in very little appreciation.

Every ministry has a beginning point. Family life ministry is in its infancy. The call for ministers and church leaders rings forth, and until recently, few answered. Pioneering is risky business. As I discovered with that lawn I mowed, you often can't see rocks, curbs, and fire ants—to say nothing about the difficulty of going in a straight line.

Churches need family ministers willing to create dangerously. The models are few and far between. The models of ministry will be built in the coming decades, and they must be built by churches willing to risk ministry. They must be built by ministers who understand the entire change process in the local church. Families are hungry for creative answers. Pat answers and platitudes will not suffice.

Churches need leaders willing to be innovators. Because this ministry is new, many churches will shy away from this effort. Some churches want to rely on historically successful programs. Other churches watch the trends in ministry and implement new ministry paradigms fairly early. None of these churches will be the seedbed for the best model. Innovative churches are looking to create a new ministry model. They have the security to make mistakes and take the heat of criticism that always accompanies the work of pioneers.

Churches need a variety of models. When people call for consultation in family ministry, I always encourage them to visit a model ministry. Even though very few exist currently, nothing affects us like the real thing. Family ministry will be different in each location and under the leadership of each minister. The field needs more models and a continuing dialogue among practitioners.

What It Can Mean to a Church

Family life ministry will raise to a new level of awareness the corporate pain and the uncovered secrets of many families. Some church systems will bear up under the strain; others will buckle. Many will sense the impending difficulties and choose to pass on establishing this ministry.

But for the church and minister willing to deal with their own issues, willing to look people in the eye and say, "I don't know all the answers, but I am here to cry with you," a new definition of valid, God-blessed ministry awaits.

What can family ministry mean in the life of the local church?

- *Blending edification and evangelism.* Family ministry is a natural way to blend two of the major missions of the church into one compatible ministry. A needs-based ministry naturally includes attention to the social, emotional, and physical needs of people and also addresses the spiritual condition of the home and family.
- *Establishing a Christian community.* The church should be a place of forgiveness, understanding, and confession. It should be the best place in the world to be in trouble. People must be put into natural contexts where deeper levels of communication can take place.
- *Developing leaders.* Family ministry begins and ends with effective leadership. The workplace, marriage, and relationships with children all benefit from men and women who understand the nature of servant leadership.
- *Upholding biblical relevancy.* Family ministry will thrust the reality of the world we now live in through every classroom and pulpit. Simple, honest communication on contemporary themes will be promoted. The comment will often be heard, "I never knew that was in the Bible!"
- *Communicating community concern.* Neighbors discover, "This church cares about folks!" Most unchurched people I visit with believe church members are interested only in themselves. When they learn we are concerned about them and their family struggles, the barriers start to come down.

- *Preparing for stress points.* Valid ministry prepares God's people for death, sickness, conflict, and many other life stresses. The church becomes a training lab for the untaught curricula of life.
- *Guidance at crisis points.* Statistics continually show that in times of stress, people will first turn to a minister. The need for effective biblical guidance is clear. Family ministry encourages competent and responsible counsel that is biblical and speaks to families as systems.
- *Using diverse talents.* Family ministry calls on the talents of men and women whose gifts often go unrecognized in the local church. The real estate agent, the marketing expert, and the songwriter may find their gifts used for the first time.
- *Opening the pulpit and classroom.* As preachers and teachers address contemporary themes from a Christian context, our auditoriums begin to ring with an authenticity that may have been missing for a long time. Church leaders are seen as shepherding costrugglers. Dialogue can begin that is the starting point for long-term change in the lives of families and in the life of the church.

As you study family ministry and read this book, remember that I am not proposing a trend or a fad in ministry. Ministering to families is not an option for ministers—it is something they will do well or not so well, but it is something they will do!

Beginnings

The start-up of a family life ministry is critical in its long-term effectiveness. As in building a house, you get only one opportunity to pour the proper foundation. It makes sense to spend time in thorough planning before heading into the implementation phase. The bulk of this book will be related to effective planning rather than lists of ideas that could be implemented.

Family life ministry should begin by focusing on several major areas: (1) uniting the leaders; (2) setting goals; (3) evaluating the congregational history and rules; (4) taking initial steps to launch the ministry; and (5) informing and involving the congregation.

Let's explore the role and relationship of each task to the launching of a new ministry. With the positive completion of each task the church can be confident of having laid the proper foundation.

Step 1: Uniting the Leaders

Although it is true that the most effective ministries are those that are "owned" by the members, family life ministry will not survive in the local church if it is not supported by the leaders. Without this commitment the ministry will struggle with problems of resources, finances, time, and integration. It will not be able to move the church to a family of faith fellowship.

Ministerial support is vital to launching the young ministry. When the minister supports family life ministry counseling, I believe church members sense they can put the trust of their most sacred struggles in the hands of the family life minister. A minister who speaks in real-life terms of the problems in the home generates confidence that the minister is sympathetic to the lives of the members, and the family ministry can speak with authority to each person's life.

The minister who supports family ministry, helps redefine families in the church, and shares personal struggles will go a long way to build an effective foundation for family ministry. The minister who "allows" the ministry to get started without support is dooming the effort to a long uphill climb.

Support must also come from the elders, deacons, and ministry leaders of the church. Church leaders must publicly support the initiation of ministry to families. They must articulate it. A written announcement delivered with all the excitement of a visit to the gas station will not convince church members. People know when leaders have something to say that they are concerned about. A sincere fireside chat by church leaders is essential in the development of the family ministry.

Ownership and support must come from the existing ministerial staff. Because integration is an important part of the ministry, and because the models are very new, it is crucial that staff ministers support the launch. Staff ministers may need help to see how family life ministry is a part of the work of the church.

Leaders must set the pace. They must unite to communicate to the church the priority of Christian family life in planning and programming. When this occurs, the ministry will take off much more rapidly than if it has to build support, justify its existence, and fight internal leadership battles.

Step 2: Setting Goals

Family ministry involves setting appropriate goals and objectives based on the evaluation of family needs. (So important is this one aspect of the ministry that we'll discuss it more in other sections of the book.)

Some church leaders turn to family ministry out of desperation. They want something done; they just don't know what they want accomplished.

Family ministry calls for setting reasonable goals. No church or institution can meet all the needs of all the people. There must be a prioritization. Some churches minister through an approach in which they put many ministries on line, hoping some new prospect will garner interest. Offerings lack depth and content. Resources are stretched, and results reign supreme.

Family life ministry takes another approach to ministry. Goals are carefully evaluated and selected. Programs are designed with quality, excellence, and a long-term impact in mind. The programs and ministries may be offered to a variety of interested audiences. Results are measured in a multidimensional manner.

Setting goals will focus the ministry on worthy objectives. It will define the use of resources, time, money, and people. Finally, it is the only way to ensure that you are truly building a needs-based ministry.

Step 3: Evaluating Congregational History and Rules

Most churches that decide to initiate a comprehensive family life ministry will have some degree of congregational history. That is, the people, events, and family rules of the past will shape the effect that family ministry will have on the life of the church. An effective leader will do well to stand the church in front of a mirror and take an honest look at how families are cared for in the congregation.

What Do You Do with Your Wounded?

One leader told me, "Don, we want this church to be the best place in the world to be in trouble!" What the church does with hurting people says a lot about who it is in Christ. The church that has consistently shot its injured sheep is not going to suddenly start bandaging wounds just because an announcement is made or a staff minister is hired. Changes can be made, but sometimes they are painful and slow. However, a church that radiates a caring concern and seems as warm and comfortable as an easy chair by a fire will easily assimilate the concepts of family life ministry.

What Are the Congregational Family Rules?

We will discuss congregational systems analysis in some detail later. Realize that each church system has rules about families. Which families are acceptable? Which ones are unacceptable? Which struggles can you pray for? Which ones do you sneak out to Jerusalem for? Does the church allow for individual differences in patterns of attendance, giving, and use of gifts? If the local church is a Christian social club, family ministry will identify people with problems who will then be socially screened out by the vast majority of the congregation. They will be left as spiritual orphans.

Do You Run Through Leaders and Ministries?

Some church leaders operate on the hope that they can stimulate involvement and commitment by continually offering new and exciting programs for the members.

They have forgotten the people. Realistic and hurting, the vast majority of the core members have seen the turn of events before. The minister may change from year to year, but given a little time, the program will be packed up and moved. It is better to sit tight and make no real commitments.

Look at the track record of ministers. Do you care for their families? Do you offer them a challenge to build a life and ministry with you? Do you protect their family time and commitments? A church that treats its ministers and ministries like interchangeable batteries will eventually treat its members in the same way.

If you really want to know how your church treats its families, ask the spouses of the leaders. Talk to the spouses of the ministers and leaders past and present about the church as a family. If you hear messages about respect, honor, and care for the leader and the family, your church likely knows how to care for its families. However, if messages of frustration, burnout, and resentment are repeated, you will immediately know that the core of the church will need ministry before any outreach can be done.

What Have Been the Major Events?

Most families can retell the stories, good and bad, that represent their history. Churches are the same way. Ask members, "What have been the most important events in the life of this church to you?" If you ask enough people, you will begin to hear the corporate congregational history.

This history is vital in understanding the people and their view of ministry. Do they remember only the bad times? Do they recall the good days gone by? Have they been searching for a dream ever since the beloved founding minister left? Are they a people with a diffused identity or a well-defined one?

All histories include positive and negative events. However, a congregation that is stuck in poor past memories will need time to heal. Family ministry may be just what the doctor ordered. The focus will need to be on internal healing. The minister will need to bind the wounds of the people and assist them in overcoming their disillusioned dreams. Only then will the minister be in a position to challenge them to meaningful outreach.

A final area of research in past history includes the personalities and belief systems of the past leaders. Every institution is shaped by the people who serve it. What have been the messages on the family delivered in the past ten years? Who have the leaders been, and what were their families like? Did their kids grow up and go to church there or stay faithful at all? Did they hide or keep congregational secrets from the church that surfaced later, leaving a residue of resentment and anger? A look at past and present leaders will go a long way in answering the question about how family ministry will fare in a congregation.

Step 4: Taking Initial Steps to Launch the Ministry

During the initial year of the new ministry, the family life minister would be well advised to take several steps to ensure the takeoff does not bounce down the runway. These recommendations will help to build credibility for the ministry.

Designate a Champion

Every ministry needs a person who is the heart and soul of the effort, someone who will put spark into the vision. Logically, this would be the family minister, but in a church that cannot afford a full-time person, this could easily be another staff person or leader.

This champion must articulate and personify the dreams and goals of the ministry. The person must champion the cause of the family in all areas of church life. The positive leadership will set the pace for the development and confidence level of the ministry. Ideally, this person should be well read in the literature and capable of communicating in large and small group settings.

Don Shultz is a great Christian friend and leader who worked for Ford Motor Company for many years. He took early retirement from a very rewarding career to devote himself full-time to family life ministry. He retrained in counseling skills, authored a ministry plan of action for his church, and helped initiate the North Atlanta family life ministry. More important, when people of that church think of a wise Christian shepherd, they turn to Don. He is a quiet champion, one man who decided he could stand in the gap in the fight for the American family and do something.

Later on, we will discuss the use of volunteers and committee organizations. However, someone needs to catch the vision of family ministry right out of the gate and be willing to infuse the leadership and membership of the church with enthusiasm and commitment. No one was ever motivated to pioneer by a committee. Family ministry needs men and women with the gift of leadership.

Cultivate Interest Among Leaders

I rarely find a church leader who cannot identify with some phase of family life ministry. Leaders are motivated by various aspects of the ministry. Some are excited about providing counseling. Others like the idea of young families receiving help with parenting skills. Still others take pride in the fact that the church is involved with the community.

As you listen to leaders' dreams, you'll hear various themes repeated. These are clues to what is motivating them to minister to families. Put these comments high on the list of priorities, and make them a part of the informal family needs analysis.

Begin with Sure Winners

Begin with classes and offerings that appeal to a wide range of people and more generic areas of struggle. Classes on communications, faith and the family, conflict resolution, and parenting will hit many common needs and create a sense of confidence and goodwill.

This is not to say that a class or group on more specialized needs should not be initiated early on. Sometimes these groups can evolve out of more general offerings. For instance, during the first year of ministry, we offered a general grief support group called Overcomers. The group worked for thirteen weeks. Out of that group came the need for a group for the divorced, parents who had lost a child, and those suffering from the more traumatic impact of long-term grief. We then made plans to respond to those needs in a more specific way.

Emphasize Quality

Quality programs and offerings must be the hallmark of any family life ministry. It is much better to start with one or two basic offerings and programs in the initial year and do them successfully than to strike out in ten different directions.

You are dealing with the most sensitive needs of people. Follow-up on community guests must be conducted with timing and courtesy. Good records should be kept of the first year of operations to document the effectiveness of all programming. Documentation should not be limited to quantitative head counting, but should include the qualitative aspects of the ministry. Are you using people's gifts? What new messages are you communicating to the church? Many measures of congregational health and ministerial success are not limited to how many showed up for the Monday night parenting class.

Put Teaching at the Forefront

As the family life minister, you are first and foremost a teacher. Your job is to teach on all levels of the church, on topics including the basics of Christian family life and effective management techniques. You must train others to shoulder the growing ministry. The massive job of teaching—from preaching to mentoring—will never end. Take every opportunity in the initial launch to rotate formally and informally through each age group in the church. Regularly visit Bible classes, small groups, and children's classes to teach, listen, and learn.

Discover Who Is on Board

You should discover who is behind this new effort, who is hesitant and needs some personal attention, who is against the effort, and who is sitting on the fence. Family ministry requires congregational commitment and cooperation. If you believe everyone will jump on the bandwagon, you may be disappointed.

Listen to the real questions that people are asking. Some people are afraid of family ministry because it involves change, and they don't like change of any kind. Rather than ignore the problem, an effective ministry should open up a dialogue between parties and seek to build consensus.

Check Out What Others Are Doing

Building a network to church and community resources is an important task in the first twenty-four months of ministry. Visit other churches and community agencies. Talk with day care directors. Meet men and women in private practice and hospital settings. My experience has shown that professionals in public and private settings are thrilled to find a church concerned about families. Pay a visit, or have lunch and discuss their work. A brochure or business card may open the door to referrals and a long-term relationship.

While working in Dallas, I met the owner of a new small Christian bookstore opening about the same time as our center. I sent him customers interested in purchasing recommended books, and he sent us families in distress. He would come in each year and set up book displays for our members at reduced prices. When I left, he was one of the largest bookstore dealers in the state and had helped network our ministry to literally hundreds of people. He served the family ministry faithfully and gave our church a positive community image.

Keep Direct Access to the Congregation

The congregation must be well informed about launching the new ministry. The ministry champion is the best person to accomplish that. Trying to convey the essential announcements regarding the ministry through secondhand sources is risky.

You should secure and keep direct access to the congregation. During one fund-raising campaign, we attempted to raise money through announcements. The money trickled in. Finally, I volunteered to address the church. Armed with a handful of pink message slips, I read off two days' requests for help that would go unanswered if we did not renovate our counseling center. The contributions rose dramatically in one week with that one five-minute appeal.

Step 5: Informing and Involving the Congregation

Congregational information and involvement are essential to the success of family ministry for three major reasons. First, through involving the congregation from the very beginning, you develop a long-term ownership of the ministry. It becomes a commitment on the part of the church. Second, involvement leads to participation. When I have ownership, I will be more likely to be involved. The congregation is not only a body to be served but also a body to be trained to serve families. Third, open information leads to fewer misunderstandings as you get farther down the road. Questions concerning the direction of the ministry can be answered cleanly when you can point to a period of time when the congregation was informed.

Rule #1: Assume People Are Not Listening

This may not be the case, but if you operate from the assumption that you have to grab and hold people's attention, a larger number of people will understand the message.

Rule #2: Use Multiple Channels

Many forms of communication are necessary to launch and maintain the ministry. In the first year of ministry I rely on questionnaires, surveys, informal coffee visits, past records, special announcements, and newsletters, to name only a few methods. Even at that level, I assume many will not understand the direction of the ministry.

Rule #3: Capitalize on Formal Communication Channels

Formal communication channels are the typical mechanisms that are in place to communicate with the congregation. They may include the church bulletin, an announcement sheet, and a parents' letter from the church day care center. Capitalize on each existing communication channel to inform people about the direction of the ministry.

Rule #4: Use Informal Communication Channels

The informal communication network might be a well-established church secretary who knows everyone in the congregation. Some information might be most effectively communicated through the church bulletin, but at other times a fifteen-minute visit in the secretary's office may accomplish the same thing. It all depends on what you are trying to accomplish.

Summary

I have had the enjoyable experience of entering a congregation where the steps I have described in this chapter have been followed.

The leaders were open with the people in setting goals. They discussed as a church family the implications of beginning a family life ministry. They counted the cost to determine if they had the resources to support the ministry. They looked at themselves and their history to determine areas of strength and weakness. After they took those steps, they set general ministry goals and looked for a minister to match the congregation and the mission.

Like a good meal, a family life ministry takes a great deal of preparation. Preparation should include strategic planning and spiritual renewal. As one church leader put it, "The preparation for family ministry should be bathed in prayer." Too often we try to move the church into new areas of ministry without making the proper preparation. The ministry fails, the people are discouraged, and vital resources are wasted. Time taken on the front end to plan properly will result in a solid foundation for the ministry.

2

THE BIBLICAL BASIS FOR FAMILY LIFE MINISTRY

The church had gathered for their quarterly business meeting. The smell of coffee and doughnuts filled the air.

"This morning we would like an update on the progress of our new family life ministry," said the pulpit minister, who chaired the meeting.

The plans for the expansion of educational classes were discussed. The need for additional counseling staff and a larger referral base was offered. The results of the needs analysis were reviewed once again for future planning purposes.

Everyone seemed pleased, except one deacon who had been squirming in his chair. He finally blurted out, "I appreciate all the noble efforts made by this staff and congregation to meet family needs. No one is more supportive of the Christian family than I am. But I will be so glad when we can get all these family problems behind us and get back to real church work again."

A long awkward silence followed. That afternoon the family minister received a phone call from a deacon's wife. She was at her wit's end, and their family was falling apart. But her husband was busy doing the work of the Lord.

Holistic Ministry

Jesus told the story about a traveler who fell into the hands of bandits. Beaten and bruised, he was left for dead. Two religious people passed him by, but a fellow from the opposite side of the tracks offered him life again. He took the injured man in, paid his bills, and was quietly on his way once again.

The story of the good Samaritan has many worthy applications. Love, charity, benevolence, and true religion are lessons illustrated by this amazing story. But the good Samaritan teaches New Testament Christians an important lesson that the Jews took for granted—the concept of holistic ministry.

The Jews understood that if people aspired to be righteous or religious, they better be ready to help their neighbors in any way possible. Pure religion meant caring for the physical, emotional, intellectual, and spiritual needs of others. Leaving out any area of need was criminal. It was a mark of spiritually immature people.

Today, Christians are warned against ignoring human suffering. "Depart in peace, be warmed and filled" is not considered an option on a multiple choice question of Christian ministry. Christians are commanded to "love your neighbor as yourself." This means concern for all needs.

The pain in families is so great that they are open and eager to hear any word from God. Simply put, when people make enough of a mess out of their lives and when the chosen answers in a society are seen not to work, portions of that society begin asking the "God questions" once again. We live in such a time.

We also live in a period of history when Christians are shrinking back from interaction with the world. Perhaps that is a normal human response to suffering, but it is not a godly one. Some religious movements are comfortable with the intellectual needs of people. They reason and debate with individuals through the best of arguments. Some groups are comfortable with the physical needs of people. If someone needs a hand, they are there from dawn to dusk. Other groups are comfortable with the spiritual needs of people. They are ready and willing to call us to the highest level of spiritual expression possible.

All these strengths are admirable and necessary. The problem defines itself when the suffering of the community and church falls into the emotional realm. Personal and family problems tend to be messy emotional situations that cannot be solved by a twenty-five-page tract in the foyer. Rather than engage the struggle, many churches shrink back in fear.

Some people, like the deacon in the business meeting, fear that if the church engages the struggles of the family, the effort will somehow water down the real mission of the church—to seek and save lost people. This reaction is tragic. It illustrates a lack of understanding about the mind of Christ and the powerful persuading influence that relationships with God can have.

Ministers must realize that people are hungry for meaningful relationships. They want good relationships with God, their spouses, their kids, and their employers (or employees).

The need for edification in our churches is increasing at an alarming rate. Church families are in desperate need of teaching, training, discussion, clarification, analysis, questioning, reading, demonstration, argumentation, and confrontation on the family issues of the day. They have placed the church in the resource provider role, and I think too many churches have remained silent.

Edification is a worthy and valued task for the local church. Through it, we Christians grow and mature in their walk with the

Savior. I believe that, too many times, young Christians are left to solve complex family problems with very little assistance from the local church. I feel that, in other cases, mature Christians never consider their need for continued spiritual development.

Many churches today would experience renewed growth by retaining the members they lost during a family crisis. This is an issue of edification, not evangelism. Movements that draw members quickly and then lose them out the back door are too busy getting more members. They do not have time to minister to the members they already have. The deacon at the opening of the chapter illustrated this principle perfectly. He was afraid. Afraid the church might not grow. Afraid the evangelistic body count would not be high enough. Afraid of what was occurring in his own house.

Family ministry is not antievangelistic. It provides one of the most natural avenues to share honest faith from person to person and from family to family. I believe that was the New Testament pattern. It doesn't release Christians from the responsibility of ministering to the holistic needs of prospects or young Christians.

Perhaps the failure in our ability to motivate people to be evangelistic, our failure to retain new converts, our failure to keep younger generations in the church, and yes, even our failure to raise honest worship to God our Father can be traced to a failure in relationship skills, not methodologies.

The church needs relationship skills. My college English professor said that *relationship* comes from the root word meaning "to create a connection again." I believe our churches, and we as ministers, must learn to create that connection again with God. We must give up the approaches to ministry that try to treat only the spiritual aspects of people and ignore all the other aspects of life. We must enter the battle, as the good Samaritan did, at the point where the pain is felt.

Jesus does not tell us about the dialogue between the traveler and the Samaritan upon his return to the inn. But I bet that traveler had some probing questions to ask that man about his values, his life, and the truths he lived by.

In this chapter we are going to explore the biblical basis for family life ministry. We will consider eight key principles necessary for establishing the biblical foundation of family ministry. The principles are evident in the pages of the Old and New Testaments. They reflect the life and teachings of Christ, His apostles, and the great characters of faith. As we walk through these passages, I hope you will see that family ministry is a natural part of the entire relationship God had with people from the very beginning. It is a contemporary application of ministry ideals that are as old as the Bible itself.

Principle 1: Family Life Ministry Practices Salvation by Association

The biblical story is a drama of humankind's lost relationship with a loving God. God acts as the initiator to reestablish His relationship as eternal Father through the saving work of Jesus Christ.

Paul wrote the Galatians,

> But when the fullness of the time had come, God sent forth His Son, born of a woman, born under the law, to redeem those who were under the law, that we might receive the adoption as sons. And because you are sons, God has sent forth the Spirit of His Son into your hearts, crying out, "Abba, Father!" Therefore you are no longer a slave but a son, and if a son, then an heir of God through Christ (Gal. 4:4–7).

God has practiced salvation by association. That is, He has chosen to deal directly and personally with fallen humankind to redeem us through the cross of Jesus Christ. God did not send a manual; He did not issue a proclamation; He did not even give us a new and improved law of Moses. He came in the flesh to deal with us.

Paul spoke to the Athenians and called their attention to the altar "TO THE UNKNOWN GOD." He reminded them that the one true God "is not far from each one of us" (Acts 17:27).

Salvation by association implies that the one trying to help joins the struggler in pain. The book of Hebrews tells us that Jesus was "in all points tempted as we are, yet without sin" (4:15). He joined us in our pain so that we might join the pain of the cross.

This is the most powerful modeling in the universe. The highest being divesting Himself of His eternal throne to join us in our disappointments. He draws us clearly to a higher standard of living, but only after telling us of His unconditional love demonstrated by Jesus' ministry.

Some folks have tried for years to build the kingdom on a mixed-up formula of ministry. I call it salvation by segregation. The reasoning is understandable. It goes like this: with all the evil in the world, perhaps it would be best for us to dissociate ourselves from the culture to live the purest lives possible. By being holy, we will be a light to the lost and draw all people to Jesus Christ.

The reasoning sounds good, and we certainly must be called to holy living, but it leads to an abuse that hamstrings the church. When we separate ourselves from the world so far that we cannot understand people's struggles or cannot identify with their pain, our religion will be perceived as irrelevant. People are open to biblical teachings on the family if they are assured of being loved and safe first.

A minister hosted a phone-in radio talk show in his town. People would call and discuss all sorts of problems. One night a young woman called to say her marriage was in trouble and she needed help. The next day the minister called a preacher at a church close to the woman's home and asked the man to visit with her. Some time later the two ministers met. "How did the meeting with the young woman go?" the first minister asked. "All she was interested in was talking about her marriage that was falling apart," the second minister replied. One man understood the power of salvation by association; the other could not.

The Pharisees offer us a classic illustration of ministry by segregation, not association. Even their name meant "the separated ones." They believed the people of God should remove themselves from the contaminating influences of the world. But they let the pendulum swing so far that Jesus accused them of being hypocrites and out of touch with people. They defended their position by complaining that Jesus was a "friend of the tax collectors" who ate with sinners (Luke 7:34; 5:30).

This contrast in ministry styles is clearly presented in John's account of the woman caught in the act of adultery:

> Then the scribes and Pharisees brought to Him a woman caught in adultery. And when they had set her in the midst, they said to Him, "Teacher, this woman was caught in adultery, in the very act. Now Moses, in the law, commanded us that such should be stoned. But what do You say?" This they said, testing Him, that they might have something of which to accuse Him. But Jesus stooped down and wrote on the ground with His finger, as though He did not hear.
>
> So when they continued asking Him, He raised Himself up and said to them, "He who is without sin among you, let him throw a stone at her first." And again He stooped down and wrote on the ground. Then those who heard it, being convicted by their conscience, went out one by one, beginning with the oldest even to the last. And Jesus was left alone, and the woman standing in the midst. When Jesus had raised Himself up and saw no one but the woman, He said to her, "Woman, where are those accusers of yours? Has no one condemned you?"
>
> She said, "No one, Lord."
>
> And Jesus said to her, "Neither do I condemn you; go and sin no more" (John 8:3–11).

Jesus' method of evangelism followed three steps. First, He brought unconditional acceptance. When the woman was placed before Him, He did not join in the ridicule of the masses. He accepted her as a human being as worthy of ministry as her accusers. Second, He delivered healing to her on a level appropriate to her pain. In the degrading situation, He refocused the attention first to Himself and then later to the religious leaders. He spoke to her kindly and let her know He genuinely cared about her. He did not make the standard religious response the woman was accustomed to. Finally, after He had accepted her and delivered a measure of emotional healing, Jesus challenged her to a higher level of living. He was not content that she continue in her sinfulness any more than He was content that the religious leaders continue in their hypocrisy.

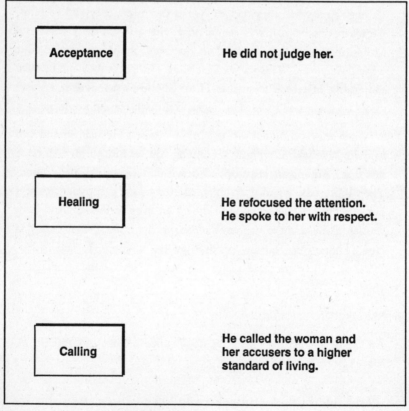

Fig. 2.1. Salvation by association

Figure 2.1 illustrates the principle of salvation by association in this case.

This beautiful story illustrates the power of family life ministry. Families that have not entered the church before will walk in and sit down when they see the church ministering to their hurts and pain. Church members will be proud to tell the community about their church: "We have something that really is meaningful to our unchurched friends."

Consider the route the Pharisees opted for. They practiced salvation by segregation. They called for the woman to suffer the harshest consequences of the law. The Pharisees turned Jesus' model around. First, they called people to higher standards of living. Please note, they were not God's standards. The Pharisees promoted the idea: "Follow all our rules and then, maybe, you can be in the club." Second, once people followed all the rules, perhaps the Pharisees would accept them—but only on a highly sophisticated ladder of spiritual superiority.

The New Testament never records that the Pharisees engaged in the work of caring for and ministering to the needs of the house of Israel. They were too busy climbing their spiritual ladders.

Salvation by association is a powerful force in any church or community. It restores an ingredient to the kingdom that I think has been lost in our latter twentieth-century church. That ingredient is relationships. People are hungry for relationships. That is why family ministry is so powerful in the community. It addresses training in the areas of marriage, parenting, and death, to name just a few. Evangelism occurs naturally out of a trust relationship among family members and friends.

The power that the woman felt from Jesus was not the relief from death or public embarrassment. It was the cleansing of a soul. It was the realigning of a life. It was the instilling of values. The power she felt was a soul being reunited with her Creator. That is the power of salvation by association. And that power is the basis of family ministry.

Principle 2: Family Life Ministry Practices a Needs-Based Ministry

I taught family relations in a community college for five years. It was my task to relate Christian family concepts to adults coming back to college to finish their undergraduate or master's degree. We met weekly for an intensive ten-week period. Most of my students came directly from work and were exhausted by the time they got to class. Keeping them awake was a challenge!

A remarkable thing occurred almost every semester. My students got really excited about the subject matter. They read their textbooks and eagerly joined in the class discussions. Many asked if they could bring their spouses to sit in on the class. Often my older students commented, "I just wish I had this information when I was raising my family."

Why all the enthusiasm? It was not the instructor because after I left, the enrollment remained high for the course. It was the subject. The topics we discussed were hitting people right where they lived. We were practicing what I call a needs-based ministry, meeting people where they are with reasonable, godly wisdom that is relevant to their daily lives.

New Testament scholars look at the gospel of Matthew as a collection of five major teaching sessions of Christ. It seems to be an instructional manual on the life and ministry of Jesus.

In the final teaching session Jesus is on the Mount of Olives with His disciples. They come to Him privately and ask about the time of His return and signs of the end of the age.

Jesus begins discussing the signs. He tells them that the day and the hour are unknown, even to Him. He relates the parable of the ten virgins. Then He makes a remarkably profound statement about the final judgment:

Then the King will say to those on His right hand, "Come, you blessed of My Father, inherit the kingdom prepared for you from the foundation of the world; for I was hungry and you gave Me food; I was thirsty and you gave Me drink; I was a stranger and you took Me in; I was naked and you clothed Me; I was sick and you visited Me; I was in prison and you came to Me."

Then the righteous will answer Him, saying, "Lord, when did we see You hungry and feed You, or thirsty and give You drink? When did we see You a stranger and take You in, or naked and clothe You? Or when did we see You sick, or in prison, and come to You?" And the King will answer and say to them, "Assuredly, I say to you, inasmuch as you did it to one of the least of these My brethren, you did it to Me" (Matt. 25:34–40).

The point is hauntingly clear. Each generation of God's people is laden with the mantle of ministry based upon the world of which it is a part. Jesus said, "I want My people to be ambassadors of grace wherever they go. I want them to respond as I would have responded while on earth."

I think the attitude of the righteous as pictured in this passage is fascinating. They are not even aware of the good they are doing! Needs-based ministry is second nature to them.

These verses are as relevant to us today as they were when spoken two thousand years ago. Imagine the impact. Lord, how will You judge those of us who are living in the latter half of the twentieth and the beginning of the twenty-first centuries? The answer lies in the pain outside our churches:

- "I was a single mother, and you helped my son have a father figure."
- "I was going through a divorce, and you did not turn away from me."

- "I was struggling with a daughter on drugs, and you helped me find a recovery program."
- "I was sexually abused by my father, and you helped me receive the healing I needed."
- "I was driven by ambition and money, and you helped me see God's priorities."
- "I was out of work, and you helped me with a house payment."
- "My wife and I could not talk without arguing, and you counseled us."
- "I was frightened of marrying, and you worked with my fiancé and me."
- "I was new to the city, and you befriended me."
- "I stood by my mother as she died, and you comforted me."

These are not extreme examples. They are the fabric of every family that attends church on Sunday mornings. They are the shackles of every family that does not. In crises we come to depend on God and our Christian relationships, or we suffer the loneliness of isolation.

Needs-based ministry is not selfish. Needs-based ministry is not faddish. Needs-based ministry is compassion in its simplest form. It is Christians walking through life trying to involve themselves as caring helpers with others. It is the local church saying, "What can we as the people of God do for a lost world in this place?"

It is not about a costly program, a new building, or an additional staff person. It is an attitude of the heart that cries out in pain with the world we are a part of. Too many churches and too many Christians have secluded themselves from the pain of the world around them.

Family ministry seeks to move beyond the denial of pain to an acceptance of our failures and the healing power of Jesus Christ. It challenges Christians to engage the struggles of the world in any arena we find ourselves in. It calls us to deliver compassionate ministry to the pain in our neighborhoods and in our families.

Principle 3: Family Life Ministry Pursues Credible Ministry

A woman from another town drove a long way to share her story and ask for help from me. When she finished talking, I asked her why she did not speak with her own minister. Her response was quick: "Dr. Don, if I had shared this with my minister back home, it would have blown his whole concept of the world!" She did not believe that her minister was capable of understanding her life, work, and problems.

Too many times church members have the mistaken idea that ministers are cloistered from the realities of the real world. Sometimes we inadvertently reinforce that perception. When our answers to life's problems do not resound with the reality of the world of the present and the confidence of the world to come, people label us as irrelevant.

Some ministers may attempt to insulate themselves from the pain and suffering of people by offering simplistic solutions and prescriptions to complex problems. The reasons for this approach may include lack of training, problems in personal life, and/or too many years of secluded ministry. In any event, church members feel these ministers could not possibly understand their struggles. They go elsewhere or drop out of church entirely.

Jeremiah the prophet warned of the dangers of an irrelevant ministry. He wrote a stern rebuke to the prophets and priests of his day that is still valid:

> "Because from the least of them even to the greatest of them,
> Everyone is given to covetousness;
> And from the prophet even to the priest,
> Everyone deals falsely.
> They have also healed the hurt of My people slightly,

Saying, 'Peace, peace!'
When there is no peace.
Were they ashamed when they had committed abomination?
No! They were not at all ashamed;
Nor did they know how to blush.
Therefore they shall fall among those who fall;
At the time I punish them,
They shall be cast down," says the LORD (Jer. 6:13–15).

We may not have all the training and expertise in the world. But we can all learn to listen empathetically to our suffering fellow humans. Jesus never tried to "slightly heal" people's hurts.

It is a sad commentary on modern religion that many families have walked into the church carrying heavy burdens only to be told their struggles are all in their minds or signs of spiritual weakness or God's ultimate displeasure. The prophets called Jesus the "Wonderful Counselor" for a reason. He came to teach us to listen to the pain in other people's lives. When we judge or ignore them, we deny them the ministry of Jesus Christ!

Several years ago I was asked to perform the funeral for twin infant girls who had died from heart defects shortly after birth. The young mother and father were not members of our church. Many of our church members tried to rally to their support, though they did not know them. I was particularly concerned about the mother's seemingly cold reaction. On our second visit I asked her, "Cathy, is there something that you are not telling me about all of this?"

Her eyes swelled with tears as her young husband took her tiny hand in his. "Tell him," he said.

She explained, "Well, Dr. Don, we have been members of a church. When all of this happened, several of the leaders came to us and told me that my daughters were taken from me as punishment from God for sin in my life. I have sinned, but I have never done anything horrible. My husband and I don't know how to go on carrying this pain, and we don't have a church to go back to now."

The burden the young couple carried through the darkest days of their lives was compounded by their church. The scars would never go away.

Jeremiah reminded his listeners that simplistic statements of "peace" when no peace exists are insults to sufferers and to God. I just returned home from a funeral for an infant at the church where I work. A heartbroken young couple sat in the front with a white coffin, not a lovely baby carriage, staring at them.

Next to them sat two families. One was their earthly family. They had been there to share sorrows of the death of the precious baby girl. Their other family, their spiritual family, was seven hundred members strong. They had come to say, "We take your pain very seriously. We valued the life of your little girl, though we never knew her. We will walk with you through the valley of the shadow of death because we are a faith family."

As I looked around, I saw the tears of sixty-year-old women who had lost children, too. I saw the quiet strength of men as they shouldered the sorrow of the moment. I saw young mothers weeping for their friends and counting their children a little more precious as they returned home that afternoon.

The minister said it best, "You will have an emptiness that can be filled only with your faith in Jesus Christ and the fellowship of this family who loves you." He was exactly right.

In the final analysis family life ministry is grief work. It is leaving the paths of comfortable ministry and becoming vulnerable to be hurt time and time again. The pain and suffering from deaths, divorces, illnesses, and accidents mount with the passing years. But if we hide ourselves behind sterile ministry that refuses to weep with those who weep, we will build a religious kingdom, but we will not build the kingdom of God.

James summed it up best:

What does it profit, my brethren, if someone says he has faith but does not have works? Can faith save him? If a brother or sister is naked and destitute of daily food, and one of you says to them, "Depart in peace, be warmed and filled," but you do not give them the things which are needed for the body, what does it profit? Thus also faith by itself, if it does not have works, is dead (James 2:14–17).

Credible ministry is servant ministry. It is ministry that begins with people and brings them to the grace of God in Jesus Christ. It is demonstrated in the lives of faithful servants in each generation, men and women who are willing to be offered up at the altar in sacrifice to the cause of Christ.

Jesus demonstrated credible ministry when on the night He was betrayed, He washed the feet of all the disciples. He even washed the feet of His betrayer, Judas. Family ministry washes the feet of families who are in crises and those who are not. John 13 is a powerful picture of credible ministry and a challenge for us to model.

Principle 4: Family Life Ministry Builds the Church as a Faith Family

Jesus' mother and brothers visited Him while He was teaching in a crowded home. When told of their arrival, He said, "Who is My mother, or My brothers? . . . Here are My mother and My brothers! For whoever does the will of God is My brother and My sister and mother" (Mark 3:33–35).

It sounds like a tough rejection from an uncaring son. But an examination of the context reminds us that Jesus' relatives were there on a mission. Word was out that Jesus had lost His mind. He was running all over the countryside saying and doing strange things.

In ancient times, a family could not have a mental health warrant issued and a family member picked up by the local authorities for examination. They went to take charge of Him. Jesus used the occasion to redefine the family in kingdom terms.

Jesus defines anyone who will do the will of God as family. Later He calls His followers friends and even brothers in the kingdom. Paul describes us as coheirs in the body of Christ.

Jesus understood the importance of close relationships in the church. He knew that when He left, His tiny band of followers was going to be subjected to persecution. Many would have family relationships severed when they became members of the church. Others would lose their standing in the local community or be expelled from the synagogues. The consequences of faithful obedience were serious.

Jesus also knew that His followers needed a place of belonging. They needed a new home that provided acceptance, love, and nurturing care, especially during times of persecution. That new family was the kingdom of God He preached about so often. The biological ties were important, but there was to be a higher plane of Christian relationship—the faith family!

Mary, the mother of Jesus, is offered as a test case for this faith family by the writer Luke. Consider Mary at the beginning of his gospel. She is pictured as a faithful servant willing to participate in the divine plan as the mother of the Messiah. She sees all the great events associated with His upbringing, the shepherds, the flight to Egypt, the temple experiences. Luke tells us she "kept all these things and pondered them in her heart" (2:19).

Then her son's ministry begins. He is rejected at Nazareth. The whole town is buzzing behind her back. She and Jesus' brothers are rejected next when they try to visit Him. Her role and status change as the mission of the Messiah unfolds. Yet hanging on the cross, Jesus looks to His mother and makes certain the apostle John will care for her after He is gone.

Luke begins the book of Acts with a catalog of the followers present in Jerusalem for the Passover. We are comforted to find Mary, the mother of Jesus, in that group. Luke presents Mary as a model believer. Although a biological relative of Christ, she moves to a higher status by becoming related to Him in the family of faith.

Why is this faith family so significant? Because of the need for relationships. The family of faith is a place where relationship with God and with fellow human beings can be learned and practiced.

A family of faith is a safe place for the single-parent family to grow. A family of faith offers hope to divorced or single people or teenagers from broken families. The family of faith has boundaries that are open enough to allow the new family in town to make a home for themselves. A faith family ministers to young persons who have obeyed God, yet must return home every evening to destructive family situations.

The world is no less tough on men and women who decide to follow Christ. Persecution of some form will always follow. I remember when a friend obeyed the gospel in college. He was giving a small talk for the first time after his conversion at a local church. He was a reserved individual unaccustomed to public speaking. A large figure moved through the foyer and pressed into the crowd. He began yelling at my friend as he spoke, chiding him for becoming a Christian. Later he told me the man had been hired by his family to dissuade him from being a Christian.

The world today is in no less need of a faith family than it was two thousand years ago. And that faith family is in need of training, pastoring, and leading. The needs analysis that I do consistently reveals that church members are in critical need of training in spiritual development and faith development skills. Topics such as having personal devotional time and sharing faith with children always rank high on the concern list. People do not have to be convinced that these are vital to their spiritual lives; they just want training in the how-tos.

A faith family implies leadership as well as acceptance. When Paul wrote Timothy concerning his work with the church in Ephesus, he described an elder. Paul rattled off a list of characteristics in rapid-fire succession. But he came to one characteristic that caused him to stop dead in his tracks: "[He must rule] his own house well, having his children in submission with all reverence." Then he added a clarifying comment: "If a man does not know how to rule his own house, how will he take care of the church of God?" (1 Tim. 3:4–5).

Paul is clear in his concept of Christian leadership. The proving ground is the home. If we cannot cut it with our own families, how can we minister to the family of God? To Paul, this idea is a key factor in the identification of Christian leadership. How does that translate to the church today? Churches are seeing the value of interviewing the family when considering a new minister. Why should that practice be limited to ministers? Every church leader should first have demonstrated the capacity for Christian service at home before being selected as a leader in the church.

The concept of the faith family is extended further when we consider the role of evangelism in the early church. Paul continued in his letter to Timothy by saying, "If I am delayed, I write so that you may know how you ought to conduct yourself in the house of God" (1 Tim. 3:15). The church is God's household. The book of Acts records many family conversions. The household of Cornelius is converted. Paul pleads with Onesimus to be merciful to Philemon, his new son in the faith who ran away. The gospel is constantly penetrating the hearts and lives of whole family units who come to God confessing Jesus Christ as Savior.

This is not accidental. God's relationship with humankind has always been based on the activities of faithful families. From the days of the great patriarchs like Abraham, Noah, Isaac, and Jacob, God worked through them and their families to accomplish His will. The twelve tribes of Israel were twelve huge extended families who took great pride in tracing their genealogy to the original roots. Once again we see the impact of the faith family. It is not surprising to see the early church converting whole families: moms, dads, and kids. The family unit was a close-knit group, and faith was practiced around the family altar. The recognition of Jesus Christ as Lord offered a dynamic shift but was one that could be shared by the entire household, given the structure of ancient family faith practice.

The church is to be God's household of faith on earth. It is a large, diverse, dynamic faith family created for the care of God's people. God is the Father, Christ is the Son, and the Holy Spirit is the heavenly counselor. Within the family of faith we enjoy all the relationships of the biological family with one great exception. God's household is eternal. Our relationships in Jesus Christ will never end. Neither will the organizing principle of this household. Like the sign in a friend's kitchen that reads, "This house is built on love," so our faith family is built on an eternal love that is freely given to all through Jesus Christ.

Principle 5: Family Life Ministry Brings All Ages and Family Forms to Worthwhile Ministry

The law of Moses presented a warning to care for the needs of socially oppressed people and minister to those outside the camp culturally or economically. Moses wrote, "You shall neither mistreat a stranger nor oppress him, for you were strangers in the land of Egypt. You shall not afflict any widow or fatherless child" (Exod. 22:22–23).

The Old Testament resounds with the warning to care for these three groups—strangers, widows, and orphans. I don't believe this is accidental. God wants His people to care for unfortunate people. The New Testament carries on this theme of worthwhile ministry to all ages, races, and life situations.

Jesus was pictured as bringing together all people to worthwhile ministry. He talked with kings and commoners. Occasionally, some of His deepest theological discussions were clearly understood by common people and misunderstood by the religious elite!

John's gospel lays two interesting conversations side by side in chapters 3 and 4. Nicodemus comes to Jesus by night, confessing, "Rabbi, we know that You are a teacher come from God" (3:2). They begin the now famous discussion of the new birth. Jesus reveals that His followers must be "born again." Must I enter into my mother's womb a second time? asks Nicodemus. Jesus chides him by saying he is one of Israel's teachers but does not understand: "That which is born of the flesh is flesh, and that which is born of the Spirit is spirit" (3:6). We are not told of Nicodemus's reaction, but the Savior certainly gave him a great deal to think about.

Chapter 4 relates that Jesus is traveling through Samaria and comes to the town of Sychar. He sits down by Jacob's well to rest while His disciples go into the town to buy food. He strikes up a conversation with a Samaritan woman. Their conversation begins with a request for water, but it soon leads to much deeper issues. The nature of worship, the coming of the Messiah, and the woman's marital history are all laid bare before the astonished woman. Jesus confides His true identity to this woman at this ordinary stop in the road.

Two individuals with very differing backgrounds discuss the significance of eternity with the Son of God. Jesus does not shrink from discussing with either person the nature of the kingdom. Nicodemus comes armed with his Jewish credentials, and Nicodemus has to overcome them. The Samaritan carries her preconceived religious notions, and Jesus shatters them. Jesus elevates both people to the status of worthwhile ministry.

One of our favorite artistic pictures of Christ portrays Him surrounded by children. Several crowd Him, and one lucky child rests in His lap. The picture illustrates acceptance. Jesus did not allow others to dictate who He would minister to. Tax collectors, sinners, outcasts, and prostitutes—all got a number in His line!

Luke presents Christ in a similar fashion. One of Luke's themes is the power of God to fulfill His promises through His faithful people. The story of the coming of Jesus reminds us that God remembers people from all life situations. He not only remembers them, but also works through them. Consider the birth narrative. A childless aging priest and his barren wife are told they will give birth to a son. An unmarried virgin from a nondescript village is told she is pregnant by the Spirit of God. The King of the world is pictured lying in a manger. The birth is announced to shepherds. Two older prophets in the temple announce the opening of God's redemptive plan when Jesus is presented. Learned teachers of the law are confounded by the wisdom of a twelve-year-old.

Do you see the wisdom of God? I will work My purposes in ways you never imagined. I will use people you never dreamed would be chosen.

Family ministry is built on this principle of acceptance. This acceptance takes two forms initially. The first deals with acceptance of alternate family forms. Singles, single parents, and blended families need identity and acceptance in the local church. I believe too many pulpits ring with the message: "Let's get back to the good old days when families were intact and perfect!" Welcome to reality. Those of us who advised the spouses in those marriages know how many of them were shells held together by good intentions. We know how many of them left hidden scars on the children, requiring extensive help to overcome. I believe there has never been a perfect time to raise a family, and there never will be.

Visit the church's bulletin board, and look at the pictures of the families. Who is pictured there, and who is not? Are there many singles, young couples with children, or widows? Where are the blended families or the divorced members? If our churches convey the idea that you must be *this* type of family to be welcome here, we can be sure our members will get the message. Those not in the group will find their way to the exits. How many have left our churches because of the unwritten message: "You don't fit in here and you never will"?

How do we improve our retention of all family forms? First and foremost by listening to them. As church leaders, we must listen to the hopes and struggles of the various family forms in churches. We are much too quick to assume we understand the suffering of the blended family or the single parent. Often we generalize from one case to all cases. It is time for church leaders to rediscover the lost art of listening.

The second form of acceptance deals with the life crises that a person is permitted to acknowledge as a part of the church. Every church has an approved list. Check out the announcements and prayers and you will get a pretty good idea of the crises the congregation can deal with openly. Some congregations stick with the magic three—illnesses, deaths, and births. But how many members' lives are touched by enormous crises that are not on the approved list?

I have been fortunate to work with a group of people who are very open about their struggles. People request prayers for job situations, family members they are alienated from, struggles with addictions, and failures as spouses. These are real-life struggles and real-life cries for help. I have mounds of compassion for Aunt Thelma's upcoming gall bladder surgery. But if that is the only life crisis we are willing to accept in the local church, we will lose many people during crises.

I am not advocating that every personal issue be laundered in front of the entire congregation. It isn't wise to share all confidential information in a public setting. But a church that cultivates the atmosphere of acceptance and prayer for hurting people will solve some of the problems that church growth experts seem to struggle with. The issue is not one of numerical growth; it is cardiac growth.

I looked out the window of my counseling office one cold Dallas morning as a beat-up station wagon pulled down the drive. The woman had just dropped off her children at the elementary school across the street and was trying an illegal U-turn through my front lawn. The heavy rains had turned our lawn into a quagmire, and soon she was up to her axles. I watched the drama somewhat amused and irritated.

When she came into the center and asked to use the phone, I sent for her. She wore light clothing that offered little protection against the cold winter air. I called a tow truck and offered to give her a ride home. I'll never forget that drive back to the projects where she lived. Her eighteen-month-old sat in the car seat. She had a long gash running across both cheeks. I asked her mother how it happened. She said, "Well, where we live, the manager will not repair the roofs or the floors. My baby fell through a two-foot hole in our apartment and landed in the apartment below. She's lucky to be alive." When I dropped off the mother and child, I prayed God would forgive me for having eyes that do not see the pain that walks in front of me every day.

Family ministry is based on the model of ministry Jesus practiced. He elevated all people to levels of worthwhile ministry. He took their struggles seriously. He gained insight into their unique predicaments and then pointed them toward a loving God and a redefined spiritual life. Jesus understood the real needs of people and met them in an open, honest way.

Principle 6: Family Life Ministry Draws on the Natural Giftedness of the Body of Christ

Paul reminds us of the importance of the natural giftedness of the body:

> Having then gifts differing according to the grace that is given to us, let us use them: if prophecy, let us prophesy in proportion to our faith; or ministry, let us use it in our ministering; he who teaches, in teaching; he who exhorts, in exhortation; he who gives, with liberality; he who leads, with diligence; he who shows mercy, with cheerfulness (Rom. 12:6–8).

Family life ministry is a natural avenue for members of the church to use their natural giftedness in the kingdom. Family ministry uses people with the gifts of ministering, teaching, exhorting, giving, leading, and showing mercy. It is a broad-based ministry that capitalizes on the individual strengths of its membership.

I have listened with compassion to ministers bemoan the fact that they cannot find volunteers for their ministries. I have not had that experience in family life ministry. My experience has been just the opposite. Whenever members of the congregation understand the nature of the mission and the need for people of differing talents, they step forward and volunteer. I generally cannot keep up with all the interviews I have to use my volunteer staff. I kept a journal of all the volunteers I was working with during a seven-day period. The list included the following entries:

- An architect designing a counseling facility
- Two counselors seeing clients
- Three persons leading support groups
- A retired teacher printing brochures
- An interior designer planning counseling rooms
- A retail store manager planning dramatic skits
- A music teacher leading a men's chorus
- A worship team planning a searcher's Bible class
- A tech man producing computer-generated slides
- A computer specialist integrating an audiovisual program
- A graphics printer doing a layout for a new brochure
- A retired executive working with a premarital case
- A teacher editing and reading a parenting curriculum
- Two women helping a friend in crisis
- Two businessmen helping a colleague in trouble
- A college professor retraining as a counselor
- A newspaper reporter doing an interview
- An accounting team working out a financial package

This list reflects an ordinary week of activity. Family ministry uses the gifts of grace of church members to meet the needs of families. Christians are delighted to learn that their individual skills can meet the needs of families in the church and community. Two marketing directors in Dallas were members of our congregation. We planned a family seminar and needed to develop a marketing strategy. They volunteered to help, convened a meeting of the top brass, and put them to work on our concept. We could have never afforded that kind of brain trust, but our members had an inside track. We received an excellent marketing strategy, and the management team felt that they had been able to contribute something to society.

Every church is different. Every family ministry is unique. One church may be loaded with people helpers, counselors, and individuals with the gifts of encouragement and mercy. Another church may have strong teachers and leaders. The family minister must gauge the needs of the church and the giftedness of the members. The minister must empower the congregation to exercise natural gifts and then develop the gifts that do not come naturally to them.

Principle 7: Family Life Ministry Holds Standards High While Ministering to Fallen People

Jesus ministered to the woman who had been caught in the act of adultery. (Incidentally, isn't it fascinating that only the woman is brought to Jesus by the men?) I stated that Jesus called her to a higher level of living after offering her acceptance and healing.

Jesus did not shame people into the kingdom of God. Neither did He open the gates wide to anyone who would not count the cost of real discipleship. It was—and is—a balance of responsibility and freedom. Jesus did not condone the woman's sin; He called her to a higher level of existence. He did not approve of the judgmentalism of the religious leaders. He called them to examine their lives. The woman and her accusers walked away looking at themselves in the mirror.

God's church must be a place where fallen men and women contact the saving grace of Jesus Christ. Nothing feels better when pain and defeat surround us. We want desperately to begin again. God says to stop depending on yourself and learn to trust My Son. The church must minister to fallen people wherever we find them.

At the same time, the church must hold the standards of Christian ethics and morality high. Our society is crying for good models and an anchor in the storm. Where do we go to see good marriages? Where do we turn to see blended families that are working? Where do we look to find parents raising responsible children? The first stop should be the local church. It seeks to build strong Christian families that have learned relationship skills with one another and with God. Find a church like that and you really have found a city set on a hill!

Our cities and towns are starving for families that demonstrate the characteristics Dr. Nick Stinnett identified among healthy families over a decade ago in *Building Family Strengths: Blueprints for Action*. Communication skills, commitment, religious orientation, time, and ability to deal with a crisis are sadly lacking in many families. Many men and women enter marriage without one model of a loving husband or a committed wife. They want to do well, but they do not have the models in their minds. It's like trying to play baseball without having seen the game. They will strike out an awful lot.

The local church must hold the standards of the Christian family very high. We minister with grace and forgiveness to fallen people, but we call all to God's higher ground. The Pharisees questioned Jesus about His stand on divorce. It was a hot topic, and they were looking for a way to trap Him. Note Jesus' first statement:

Have you not read that He who made them at the beginning "made them male and female," and said, "For this reason a man shall leave his father and mother and be joined to his wife, and the two shall become one flesh"? So then, they are no longer two but one flesh. Therefore what God has joined together, let not man separate (Matt. 19:4–6).

I believe Jesus was consciously clearing the decks before He launched into His discussion on divorce. He was saying to the Pharisees that before we get entangled in all the legal debates, let's remember the original plan. Let Me raise the flag, point out the plan, and refocus the lens. God intended one man and one woman for one lifetime. That's the standard from the Father. We can talk about exceptions all day, but if folks will remember that the product comes with an instruction manual and that manual says on page one that monogamous marriage is the ideal, we ought to pay attention.

That may seem like an unpopular position to take, but the church must raise the standards of Christian family ethics as high as God intended them to be. God intended husbands to love their wives. God intended children to be born into loving homes with mature parents willing to take the responsibility for their care and nurture. God intended families to care for their aging parents. God intended sex as a wonderful gift for two people in marriage, not an athletic event for a fallen culture. God intended people to treat one another with integrity, fairness, honesty, and compassion. These are not old-fashioned concepts; these are biblical truths. We can ignore them, but the Book states our lives will be enriched when these truths are applied.

Someone may object, "All that sounds like a lot of work. Why can't family life and Christianity be easier?" Healthy families, servant-minded Christianity, and most worthwhile things in life take effort and discipline. The Hebrew writer reminds us that discipline is a part of our relationship with God:

If you endure chastening, God deals with you as with sons; for what son is there whom a father does not chasten? But if you are without chastening, of which all have become partakers, then you are illegitimate and not sons. Furthermore, we have had human fathers who corrected us, and we paid them respect. Shall we not much more readily be in subjection to the Father of spirits and live? For they indeed for a few days chastened us as seemed best to them, but He for our profit, that we may be partakers of His holiness. Now no chastening seems to be joyful for the present, but painful; nevertheless, afterward it yields the peaceable fruit of righteousness to those who have been trained by it (Heb. 12:7–11).

Building strong Christian lives takes pain and effort. It is a growth process involving disciples and God's Spirit working through their lives. It is a dynamic process producing the fruits of the Spirit including joy, hope, love, and self-control. These are the essential elements of the Christian life and the Christian family.

Paul wrote to the Philippian church that Christian growth involves a series of painful confrontations with one's identity, ultimately producing spiritual maturity. He urged them to solve their conflicts internally and repair the damaged reputation the church was building in the small community. He summarized his advice by saying, "Brethren, I do not count myself to have apprehended; but one thing I do, forgetting those things which are behind and reaching forward to those things which are ahead, I press toward the goal for the prize of the upward call of God in Christ Jesus" (Phil. 3:13–14).

Paul was saying, "I make mistakes. I am not perfect. I have a past that causes me a great deal of pain and grief. But I have a risen Savior whose memory gives my life mission. I forget the mistakes I have made and put my eyes on the perfection of Jesus Christ. When I am looking at Him, I can strain ahead, endure the pain, and grow spiritually each day."

Family ministry runs a delicate balance of ministering to the pains of suffering families and holding the standards of Christian relationships high. These are complementary activities that will motivate men and women to strive to live better lives in Jesus Christ. Our churches and communities are hungry for God's Word concerning the family. Both messages must be delivered with power, compassion, and conviction.

To raise the standards of healthy Christian relationships, the local church must be moving toward spiritual and relational health, also. Notice I said moving toward that direction. Some churches are healthier than others. They are able to communicate, celebrate, and conflict in an effective manner. Other churches suffer from various symptoms that are detrimental to the spiritual health of the body.

An unhealthy church will not produce healthy families. In such a church the family life minister becomes a change agent trying to help unhealthy families in an unhealthy church system. It is a losing battle. Until the church is willing to look in the mirror as Jesus challenged the religious leaders and the woman caught in adultery to do, it will do more harm than good to families. These churches may participate in elaborate schemes of denial. But church members and visitors can feel the reality. Staffs will change frequently, members will flee, and occasionally a group or person will be martyred to keep the focus of the church off its own issues. The goal is to not look in the mirror.

I believe the same characteristics that build strong families build strong churches. Relationships in Christ can be generalized to that level. Our churches and families need honest, open communications, times of celebration and rest, and relevant problem-solving methodologies, to name only a few. When our churches and families operate from Christ's agenda for interpersonal relationships, we will begin to build healthy churches and healthy families.

Principle 8: Family Life Ministry Builds Real Families, Not Ideal Ones

The biblical text, especially the Old Testament, gives us fascinating glimpses into the family lives of many great people. Not one family mentioned in the Old or New Testament is cast in the ideal family role. If families are so important, why didn't God provide us with one perfect or near perfect model?

Biblical families are real families. When we read the text, we often lose the feel of emotions, the pain of struggle, and the uncertainty. But they were people just like you and me. They had dreams for their children and the need to be loved.

There are no ideal families, just real families. Real families experience crises, defeat, and pain. Real families have real moms and dads with real strengths and weaknesses. Real families have imperfect children who make mistakes and don't always turn out exactly the way Mom and Dad hope they will.

But real families are all God has given us to work with this side of heaven. We must learn to minister to the real struggles of daily living. One of my favorite teachers, Dr. Carroll Osburn, states it succinctly, "The message of Jesus was given to teach us how to walk the cobblestone streets, not the streets of gold." We must not create churches where there is an illusion of perfection. Churches where only the saintly walk through the foyers and grace the halls will be very lonely places.

Our task is to join with families in the ethnic, cultural, and economic struggles of the latter years of the twentieth century. Our job is to prepare a generation of young people who will see changes and challenges in their lifetimes unknown to us. Our mission is to present a faith demonstrating a dynamic process of spiritual living that points to the Savior Jesus Christ.

In accomplishing that mission, we must be seen as constructive costrugglers in the issues of family building. This struggle is not easy. It was never intended to be. It does not produce flawless families; that is an ideal we strive for but never attain. It is a mission that accepts the imperfection inherent in each human family, yet strives for the perfection in Jesus Christ.

Family life ministry tries to help families become more reality based in their faith. Family members must learn to be real in their relationships with one another. Family members must learn to be real in their relationship with Jesus Christ. The only ideal is found in Jesus, and He alone can provide us with the power to become real with Him and one another.

Conclusion

We began this chapter with two assumptions. First, we assumed that family life ministry is holistic ministry. It addresses all the needs of people—physical, spiritual, intellectual, and emotional. Second, we assumed that family life ministry combines the two great missions of the church, edification and evangelism, in a natural way.

Based on these two assumptions, I proposed eight foundational points related to the biblical basis of family life ministry:

1. It practices salvation by association.
2. It practices a needs-based ministry.
3. It pursues credible ministry.
4. It builds the church as a faith family.
5. It elevates all ages and family forms to the level of worth-while ministry.
6. It draws on the natural giftedness of the body.
7. It holds standards high while ministering to fallen people.
8. It builds real families, not ideal ones.

The biblical basis for family life ministry is a study in Christian relationships. The Bible is filled with teachings that define and enrich our relationships in Christ. Any of these can be applied to the study of marriage and the family.

As the family life minister, you must build a solid foundation biblically for the ministry. You will need to revisit these themes frequently to help church leaders and members rethink their concept of family ministry.

3

BARRIERS TO FAMILY LIFE MINISTRY

It was a beautiful summer day in Atlanta. My wife and I had moved in a few weeks ago, and Sunday morning I preached on Christian marriage to my new congregation. Tuesday morning I phoned my insurance company to arrange for the transfer of some policies. The friendly representative who answered the phone repeated my name as if she knew me personally. *This company must really emphasize customer relations,* I thought.

"Do I know you?" I asked.

"No, but I know you Mr. Hebbard. You're the guy who told that funny story about your wife in your sermon last Sunday morning," she said.

Now I was really curious. "Were you attending our church? Are you a member there?" I asked.

"No, but I work with a lady who is, and she told us all about your sermon on families. That sounds like a church that really cares about folks!"

I don't remember if we ever got around to talking about insurance, but we did talk about her family and her desire to find a church home that "really cared about folks." For this friendly lady, the barriers to religion had come down through a brown bag lunch and a friend who cared enough to share a story.

In this chapter we will discuss some of the barriers that exist to building a ministry to families in the local church. The effort to address some of these barriers is often enormous. But the effort is worth it. Remember the insurance representative who was touched by a church that was willing to risk breaking down some of those barriers for the cause of the Christian family.

The Holy Turmoil

There is no way that a ministry dealing so directly and immediately with the heart and soul of the local church can escape a wide range of reactions. But I was poorly prepared for the variety of responses of church leaders and members to family life ministry. In my naive mind, the thought of a church ministering to the felt needs of the members and the community seemed like a godly endeavor. How could anyone not be supportive of family ministry? How wrong I was!

As a family minister, you must prepare yourself for various responses to the ministry. Some of these responses will be easily managed with time and discussion. Others will be highly emotional and charged with years of untapped pain and denial. Often, the corporate and familial pain of the church will be directed against you as the agent of change.

This chapter will focus on these questions: How are churches responding to family problems? What are the major barriers to family life ministry? Why are church members not coming to the church for help anymore? What steps can be taken to address the situation? Coming up with the complex answers to these questions will require a large portion of your time and energy during the initial years of the ministry.

A Primer on Church Responses

I have noticed through the years that churches have typical approaches to dealing with family problems. Some churches, even in the face of losing a minister due to marital difficulties, can take denial to an art form and continue business as usual. Others work through the pain and grief in a more healthy way. My assumption is that every church will experience family difficulties in the pew and pulpit at some point. What matters is the appropriateness of the congregational response.

The Ostrich Approach

Some churches bury their heads in the sand when it comes to family problems. They have acceptable and unacceptable family life crises. If a struggle falls outside the realm of acceptability, they look the other way.

Families in these churches tend to be of three types. First are the families who maintain an uneasy veneer of perfection. These are the ostriches who generally maintain control. Second are the sufferers. These are the couples, singles, teens, or children who make the mistake of having an "improper" struggle. They are politely ignored by the first group and eventually wander away, much to the relief of the ostriches. The third group includes the watchtower people. Few in number, they see the ostriches and sufferers and call for a response. They are generally tired, carry a massive pastoral load, and eventually burn out and leave.

The Ejection Approach

Some churches categorize all family struggles as wrong and communicate unbelievably high standards. When the standards are not met, these churches rid the body of the "offender." These churches tend to toss wayward sheep over the cliffs; after all, it's their own fault they got lost, isn't it?

The Mother's Day/Father's Day Approach

Some churches take a superficial approach to all family concerns: "Do we minister to our families? You bet. I preached a series on it around Mother's Day." Superficial treatments and superficial answers communicate only one message: "We don't understand you, and we aren't listening!"

Every church can develop a systematic, inexpensive approach to ministering to families. I was delighted to work with a small congregation that was working through the loss of a minister due to family difficulties. Although the members had never approached the problems before, they were determined to be credible, informed, and wise in each step they took with the minister, his family, and the congregation. They navigated a very serious event in their congregational history by resisting the urge to make quick, superficial judgments or bury the problem in denial. They arranged for counseling, gave the minister a sabbatical, were attentive to the needs of the wife and children, and helped walk the church through the painful passage. It took much time, effort, and prayer, but a church and a family were saved.

The Latest Fad Approach

I receive bulletins from churches all over the country. Some churches specialize in being the first on their block to offer the latest fad movie, program, speaker, and topic. Little attention is given to the fact that the resources may or may not be appropriate to the church members.

Church members become conditioned to a three-ring circus approach to meeting needs. They learn to sit back and watch the new show. Lives are not changed, guests from the community are not reached, and resources are wasted. But did they have a crowd last night!

The Title-Only Approach

This is probably the most disconcerting trend in ministry. I periodically receive calls from men and women wanting to enter family ministry or change the focus of their ministry toward a more family orientation. Almost without exception, when the discussion turns to retooling for ministry, they offer excuses: "Can't I just spend a day with you and get what I need to take back to our place?"

Ministers who present themselves as family life ministers must realize that they present an image to the congregation that they are trained to handle marriage and family counseling. Many ministers deny this will be the perception, but I can say emphatically that it is the perception among church members. When I take the name *family minister,* I also take on the perception of certain competencies that go with it. If the people perceive me to have the competencies, I better think carefully about my gifts and formal training.

We will discuss at length the training and competencies of the family life minister in another chapter. Let me state as clearly as I can, no church has the freedom to add family life minister to its staff list without a properly trained individual who can fulfill the expectations of the church and community.

Land Mines in the Harvest Fields

As the family minister, you will encounter many barriers to an active ministry to families. Some of these barriers originate with issues inherent in the life of the church. Others stem from unresolved issues in the personal, marital, or family life of members of the church or ministerial staff.

Predicting which barriers will exist in any given church is difficult. However, by probing with several appropriate questions, you may be able to uncover some of the larger land mines in the harvest fields. Let's look at a few of them.

The Counseling-Only Preconception

Most church leaders who discuss family life ministry with me begin with a notion of a counselor or counseling center. This is valid ministry, but it is not comprehensive family ministry because it lacks the preventive component. When we discuss the possibilities of expanding their horizons into a proactive ministry, most leaders are very excited.

In this situation you will have to work hard to reeducate the church that you are more than an on-call counselor. Ongoing dialogue with the leaders should forge out a job description that may limit the total time spent in counseling and associated responsibilities. Then you will have adequate time for developing preventive programs, training volunteers, and doing effective outreach in the community.

Integrating the Bible with Psychology

The family minister will want to base his entire ministry on a solid biblical foundation. He will also want to help the church glean many useful concepts from the fields of psychology, human development, and counseling. While the Scriptures always serve as the ultimate source of truth, other disciplines can be used to help us explain family dynamics.

For example, Ephesians 5:21 encourages us to "submit to one another out of reverence for Christ." That is the biblical mandate.

But how do we do that? That is where other disciplines can step in and illustrate how to demonstrate those behaviors in the home. How do I learn to control my temper? How do I demonstrate humility? These are questions that the study of human behavior can help answer in perfect harmony with God's revealed Word. The family minister will help the church see that the study of family systems confirms what the Bible has been saying for centuries.

Simplistic Answers to Complex Problems

I used to get a tape from a local minister and listen to it every week. His exegesis of the passage was always impressive. His speaking style was flawless. He was an orator and a communicator. But when it came to application, he had basically the same prescription every week: pray, study your Bibles, and trust God.

That's fine advice. I strongly believe that each Christian should be actively involved in prayer, Bible study, and many forms of discipleship leading to spiritual maturity in Christ. But is it wise to answer all of life's struggles with such a pat prescription? Unfortunately, he was telegraphing to the congregation the message: "I don't really understand the complex nature of your problems, and I'm certain if I did, I wouldn't know what to say. How about taking this neutral religious advice and applying it on your own and letting us both off the hook?"

That wasn't the message he intended at all. That wasn't the message the people wanted to hear. But it was the major ministerial message for pain and suffering in that church.

Remember Jeremiah's warning concerning simplistic answers to complex problems:

> Because from the least of them even to the greatest of them,
> Everyone is given to covetousness;
> And from the prophet even to the priest,

Everyone deals falsely.
They have also healed the hurt of My people slightly,
Saying, "Peace, peace!"
When there is no peace (Jer. 6:13–14).

No one can be an expert on every unique life struggle. But we must learn to sit by the wells. We must learn to get out of ourselves and our preconceived orientations and get into the orientations and struggles of the people around us.

We need to promote diligent retooling for all staff members. The problems we are encountering in families today were unaddressed a generation ago. These issues are redefining the nature of ministry. We must learn the problems before we apply the text. As we learn about the struggles of our members, we will experience an amplification of God's Word. New passages will jump out with color and clarity that we never dreamed of before. We will explore the text with creativity as helpers and costrugglers.

Denial

Denial tends to be one of the most common and pervasive barriers to family ministry. It will be associated with many other symptoms and manifestations of opposition to the ministry. Denial in church systems functions in much the same role as denial in unhealthy families. Church leaders may go to great lengths to deny and protect the ills within the church family. The family minister runs the risk of confronting the denial and becoming a scapegoat.

I was called in as a consultant to a large urban church. Families in the church were trying to do too much, and they had too many demands placed on them. The church functioned from a numerical success model of church growth in the crassest sense. Get bodies, fill balconies, and run off members who do not "fall into line." The church was worn out, riddled with difficulties, and deeply resentful.

Members felt used. They had been wrung out to fulfill the ambitious demands of power and prestige by the leaders.

When I conducted a family needs analysis, the documented need for counseling and pastoral care was remarkable. I prepared the report and met with the church leaders. After an hour's discussion, it was clear they were not concerned with the needs of their people. They simply wanted people who were willing to work hard and get with the program.

I could see that the church was suffering from denial at the highest level of leadership, which is not an uncommon situation in local church work. Leaders believe that if they can deny the problem, it is bound to go away. Instead, it grows and festers until it puts at risk the very kingdom of God in that place. They inadvertently sacrifice the very thing they are trying desperately to build.

As with many other barriers, denial often stems from the unresolved issues of the leaders, minister, and congregation. Just like a healthy family, the church must learn to forgive, confess, and navigate the crises that are a part of the life cycle of any church.

In contrast to that church's experience, I have found that a family ministry can have a dramatic impact on people's lives when problems are not denied. Research done through our ministry shows that 45 percent of the people responding to our church for prayers, for membership, or to obey the gospel have been connected with our family life ministry. Over 50 percent of fringe members whose attendance and involvement are sporadic are maintaining a tie with the church through the counseling ministry or another family life ministry program. The connection between real-life struggles and ministry is made naturally when denial is confronted.

Don't Air Your Dirty Laundry

A common belief of the "ideal family" of generations gone by was that the family handled all of its own problems. If Dad stumbled in drunk on Saturday night, the family got him dressed on Sunday morning and propped up in a pew. After all, what would the neighbors think?

This type of reasoning is still a part of some people's thinking. You must help the church rewrite some family rules in regard to the acceptability of failure and the promise of unconditional love. You must create an environment where it is safe and confidential for any member or community guest to receive help.

The Enormity and Severity of the Problems

Some church leaders are reluctant to enter family ministry due to the extent and complexity of the problems. Functioning from a denial base, they may opt to avoid the conflict entirely. Unfortunately, it usually takes a short period of time before a young couple, missionary family, or leadership couple suffers from some family need. As I have stated before, family ministry is not an option. It is something churches will do well or they will do poorly, but they will do it!

Unacceptable Crises

Most churches define what is acceptable and what is not acceptable to struggle with. Just check the response cards. Naturally, not every private sin needs to be made public, but we must regain some openness in our assemblies for members to experience what I call corporate healing.

Several years ago I worked with a Christian couple who had been longtime members of their church. They worked very hard to put their marriage back together. Because of the personalities in the marriage, many in the church knew of their struggles and their efforts to be restored to each other and to God. Both came forward at the end of one service and brought prepared statements of repentance and recommitment to God and each other. Tears flowed and prayers were offered. After church that day, they were mobbed with supportive Christian brothers and sisters who hugged, cried, and shared similar struggles. They experienced God's love and approval in flesh and blood that morning.

I have seen other folks come to churches for help. They may come forward with a beautiful statement or reach out to a small group but are met with the unstated message: "We don't allow folks with those kinds of struggles around here!" The church doesn't have to tell them twice to leave.

Quantitative Growth

Many churches that will launch family ministries will see them solely as a means to stimulate numerical growth. They want to draw crowds with the curriculum of family ministry. However, by definition, family ministry blends edification and evangelism. Churches are filled with people who are dying for the answers to *how* questions: How do I get along with my spouse? How do I raise my children to love God? How do I control my ambition?

Family life ministry seeks to apply the biblical text to the *how* questions. Certainly, we are interested in all people being reached for Jesus Christ. But many of the quick disciple-making approaches leave underdeveloped Christians struggling with issues of job, family, and the church. Family ministry calls for commitment to Jesus Christ as Savior and commitment to dynamic discipleship.

I have worked with many people coming out of what I called highly successful church models or highly controlling religious systems. Without exception their marriages and families have suffered tremendously. This is an abuse of Christian authority and in too many cases is an outgrowth of power addiction. Jesus Christ commissioned the church to do two equal functions: "Go into all the world," and "Teach them everything I have commanded." To do less is to change the gospel of our Lord.

Staff Problems

Sometimes barriers inadvertently arise from within the ministerial staff:

- *Reaction to core knowledge.* Some staff ministers may be threatened by the family ministry's ability to go almost immediately to the heart and core of the church. Knowledge base and trust can be quickly built. Talent often comes flowing to the ministry, reducing recruiting problems so common in other areas. Jealousy and territorialism can develop if staff members are not included in planning and implementation.
- *Leadership issues.* The initiation of a family life ministry in a multiple staff setting may surface some undiscovered issues or undealt with problems within the ministerial staff.
- *Resources.* As needs are identified, the family minister will urge a reallocation of resources among existing ministries. Talk about the love of God, talk about the ministry of Christ, but talk about my budget and we've got problems! Resources are scarce in any church, and the addition of a new kid on the block may shake up the old guard.

Resistance to Planning

Some churches resist planning and prioritizing. It is more fun to be busy all the time and not really consider where they are going and how they are going to get there. Family ministry, with its focus on human needs, may cause some church leaders to stiffen: "Why do we have to be so businesslike and organized? Let's just get moving!"

Family ministry may also cause leaders to ask penetrating questions concerning the effectiveness of ministries. Especially in an older, larger church with multiple programming models, it is easy to build up barnacles of ministries that ceased being effective years ago. They have retained their identity and form because of tradition or the presence of a powerful opinion leader in that ministry. Asking too many questions can be hazardous to the status quo. But as my father would say, "The status quo is fine, but if your quo has no status, you're in big trouble!"

Church as Club

I have been a member of a health club chain for many years. I work out with some guys who watch the hired help come and go. It's a chain that is interested in only one thing, selling more memberships. Employees give you all the attention you could possibly want until you put your name on the dotted line. Then you are on your own. These gym rats as we call them are salesmen. They know nothing of physical fitness and even less about sweating. They are there to make their commissions.

Some churches function in much the same way. The ministerial staff is at the front door to sell memberships. Forget a good workout in God's Word; just show up in a nice workout outfit and don't make any trouble. Having some trouble with a machine or need someone to spot you? Forget it. We're busy selling another great future member on our great church.

I would quickly add that many churches do not function in this way at all. Their warmth and hospitality are genuine. They are willing to get in there and sweat with the group. However, the family minister must be aware that the church may function as a club with members, and the minister has been hired as the fast-gun problem solver who will take care of all the problems. Such expectations are inconsistent with Christian ministry, breed immature churches, and burn out ministers and families.

Tree Stump Experts

Most churches I visit have a tree stump family expert. These experts have all the answers to all current and future family problems distilled into a condensed version. They normally take offense at the idea that some problems might be beyond their ability to tackle.

If trained, these people can become wonderful resources because of their people skills and communication abilities. If allowed to run loose, they will ultimately create more problems than they solve.

Lack of a Theological Base

Dennis Guernsey was correct in his book *A New Design for Family Ministry* when he observed that "family ministry has been built from the roof down." We do not have a comprehensive theology of the family. I hope this will be a task for the immediate future.

Family ministry evokes many theological questions concerning marriage, divorce, suffering, pain, singleness, sex, parenting, and money, to name only a few. The training of the family minister must reflect an ability to help church members with the theological implications of their lives and decisions. In coming years this should be an area of greater thinking and fruitful study.

Accessing Corporate Pain

Take an empathetic minister anxious to meet human needs, drop the minister into a conflict-ridden church, and you have an immediate reaction. Phone calls flood in, pain is shared, and wounds are opened. Many churches are hamstrung because of unresolved congregational conflict.

If you encounter such corporate pain in your church, you have three options:

1. Ignore the pain, and participate in the denial cycle.
2. Try to act as an internal consultant.
3. Attempt to facilitate negotiations through an external consultant.

The first two options are counterproductive for you and the church. Denial intensifies the problems, and trying to act as an internal consultant may be noble but is loaded with hidden dangers. I have found it almost impossible to help in that role.

The best option is for you to view the congregation as an unhealthy family in need of treatment. You should encourage the leaders to seek an outside consultant to assist in the definition and evaluation of the problems. In this way you help the church take ownership of the issues.

If the leaders are open to this option, you should assume a pastoral posture with the church. You should provide the adequate care and security needed by people going through a transitional period. Change is difficult in the best of circumstances for everyone involved. If conflict is to be successfully negotiated, you can serve in a very Christlike manner by ministering to the body during a time of great need.

Many family life ministries will face one or a combination of these barriers during the initial years of the ministry. In my own experience, it has taken years in some cases to alter deeply ingrained perceptions of members and leaders.

Some churches face a tougher uphill battle before even beginning a credible ministry to families. These churches have inadvertently taught their members that it is not safe for them to come to the church for help and counsel.

Why Don't They Come to Us for Help?

Churches have informal reputations with their members and the community. Some churches are known as safe havens in a storm. Other churches are great worshiping societies or educational institutions.

Churches also develop reputations for dealing effectively or ineffectively with people problems. One of the toughest reputations for a church to live down is the unwillingness or inability to cope with family concerns. My conversations with local church members lead me to conclude that more and more congregations are being perceived as at best irrelevant and at worst hostile to the struggles of contemporary families.

The bottom line to this situation is clear: our people are not coming to us for help. Perhaps you are the exception to the rule. My judgment is that for every call coming in to the local church, two or three more are made to other sources of help. Many times no calls are made until it is too late.

I have looked into the eyes of too many church members who complain of incompetent responses to personal, marital, and family difficulties from ministers. They state, almost as a rule, that they will never again risk vulnerability in the life of the local church. It is not a problem of the members; it reflects the way church leaders approach family ministry.

To illustrate this, let me share something that happened to a close friend. Her experiences and response reflect the growing dissatisfaction with the abilities of the local church to deal with family problems.

She was an articulate, devoted, hardworking mother who had been married almost seventeen years. Her husband, an architect, was a deacon in the church and led the fellowship committee. He was the life of the party and had many friends both at church and at work. She enjoyed a wide circle of friends in the church and community.

Rumblings of marital difficulties surfaced several years before I met the couple. The husband had been having an affair with a woman where he worked. The devastating effects on the marriage had been worked through, so it seemed, but the wife's fears of additional relationships caused her much concern.

His good-natured ways and his ability to contribute significantly to the work of the church caused most church leaders to doubt what their best instincts were telling them. They could not believe the wonderful man could be capable of multiple affairs, even though an occasional report of flirting came from women of the church.

About four years following the initial affair, the news broke that he had been involved in a whole series of sexual relationships with women inside and outside the church. The details were sordid and depressing. The family was blown apart, and the mother struggled tenaciously to hang on to her children and her faith.

Several events happened in succession that caused my friend to consider leaving the church entirely. First, the leaders of the church made no effort to contact her. Left on her own, she had the presence of mind and faith to schedule a meeting with the church leaders. Coming, as a woman, to a meeting of men was threatening enough. Through many tears, she shared the details of her marriage. She laid her heart on the table. When she was finished, no one said a word. A brief prayer was offered, and she turned and left the meeting. She was crushed.

Not long afterward, she was disturbed to discover that the details of her meeting with the church leaders were circulating among many church members. And much to her dismay, the details had been significantly changed. She was appalled to learn that many members, with whom she had little or no relationship, were running her life story on the church's unofficial news network.

The final blow came as a slow death rather than a thunderclap. People in her Bible class seemed strangely absent when she needed them most. The friends who used to call were too busy. Even her children felt removed from the youth group.

She met with me and shared her story. She told me of her husband's many sexual exploits and how she had felt like the guilty party when she shared the story with the minister and shepherds of the church. She looked me straight in the eye and said, "I will never again trust my life to the church."

I have heard this story repeated numerous times by well-intentioned members of the church. Individuals who have been brought up to believe that they are expected to come to God's people during crises vow they will never again expose themselves to the kinds of public humiliation they endured. "I will not be fodder for the women's class luncheon," one woman complained.

I ask again, Why do our people not come to us for help? The answers lie in many of the experiences discussed by my friend. Let's explore them in detail.

They have told us of their struggles, and we do not believe them.

Like the apostles running back to report the resurrection of our Lord, they meet blank stares implying, "We think you're crazy!" All forms of unethical behavior can be found in many churches. This reaction of total disbelief tells people that the leaders don't live in the world they live in every day of their lives. And we better realize that hurting members check us out! One woman came into my office and said, "I would not have come in to talk to anyone here at church about this, but my friend talked with you about something like this and she said you were safe to talk to." Churches that take an ostrich approach to family problems cannot expect to attract eagles or angels with broken wings.

They have tried our prescriptions and know they do not always work.

In our earlier discussion of simplistic answers to complex problems, I stated that the biblical text provides insights into the toughest human situations, but we as students must take the time to dig the answers out.

Church members flock to counselors complaining that the teaching and preaching are irrelevant to their struggles. They are accustomed to a world that does not provide neat and clean answers. It is not an affront to us to admit theirs may be a difficult problem, we do not know all the answers, and we are costrugglers in the search for God's will in the matter. Such a response would raise the level of believability and credibility for most ministers.

They do not view the ministers and church leaders as transparent costrugglers with life's problems.

Most of us would benefit from doing a rigorous self-examination of our weaknesses as well as our strengths. Family ministry assumes the minister and staff are willing to embrace a level of transparency.

I was coteaching a series on great doctrines of the church on Wednesday evenings. The subject for the evening was the nature of the church. My wife and I had just returned from vacation at the beach. We had been discussing our role in the church and Christianity in general.

I shared with her at that time how I felt about Christ. I had approached Jesus as an academic, as a churchman—but never as a humble disciple. I was always coming to the Cross with *my* agenda to be met. I told her I was committed to be less of a professional churchman and more of a disciple. My goal was to put Jesus at the center of my life in the most practical ways I could.

My part of the lesson was about ten minutes that night. I was to talk about the qualities of the body of Christ. Instead of sharing what I knew (my strengths), I decided to share what I did not know (my weaknesses). The group's response to that ten minutes was the best I had ever experienced.

People want to know their leaders are credible. They want to know leaders are honest. We do not have the right to place ourselves above legitimate struggle. When our churches see real struggling leaders who roll up their sleeves and get involved with the problems of the day, they will be inspired to do better themselves in their own lives. It is basic motivation by inspiration, not declaration.

We have broken confidences with them.

We must respect the privacy and confidentiality of members and community guests. No one, no matter what the position or relation, has a right to the private conversations of others, especially at church. No church leaders, staff members, or administrative support persons should be allowed to maintain their positions for one day if they tend to gossip.

The family minister may need to retrain the leaders, staff, and secretaries in the church to respect the privacy of every member and visitor. This may mean some dismissals. This may entail some confrontations. The alternative is to send the message: "If you share your story, it's everyone's story!"

The family minister must receive authority to arrange damage control for marriages and families in stressful situations. This includes recommending that certain leaders coordinate their efforts. In larger churches, often the right hand doesn't know what the left is doing, and someone must step in to monitor the aid and information. The family life minister is in the best position to do this.

We do not open ourselves to legitimate censure and supervision.

Some congregations are suffering the ill effects of church leaders and ministers who are not skilled people helpers. Some individuals seek position and power for fame and glory to bolster sagging egos. They must be in control at church because they have little or no control anywhere else in their lives—at work or at home.

Such individuals regard themselves as dynamically talented counselors. Not only has God given them the brilliant talents of leadership (defined dictatorship) and communication (defined lecturing), but He has also empowered them with insight into the complex nature of human behavior, personality, parenting, and all other family issues. The tragedy is that some church members take these people seriously. They listen to these people because of the title they carry.

A Christian counselor approached me after services one day with a worried look on his face: "Are you aware of a support group being conducted by George here at church?" Since I was new to the position, I had only heard of the group and its leader. He continued, "Well, I have had a lot of people through my office who have been given some very strange advice coming out of that group. You might want to look into it."

When I did, I was alarmed by what I found. One fellow had decided on his own to start a support group. He had no supervision, no training, and no one to report to. A few questions into our discussion revealed that he had not worked through the issues of his childhood. He was working out his own agenda on the members of his group with no accountability. When he refused counseling, training, and supervision, I closed the group down—but not before several people had been hurt by the irresponsible abuse of power.

Entering the local church is no reason for dropping our expectations regarding training, education, expertise, and supervision.

Generations ago, ministry was regarded as the highest and most revered profession. It was the profession that gave birth to all other professions, including medicine. The word *professional* did not hold the cold, distancing feelings that many people associate with it today. A professional in ministry meant that person was held accountable to a higher standard of excellence than others out of deference and authority to the Word of God.

We need to recapture that attitude. We as church leaders need to decide we are going to be the best prepared, the most responsible, and the most accountable people on earth. Not for our sake, but for the sake of the gospel.

It is time to make continuing education a mandatory requirement for all staff and church leaders. It is time to ask tough questions of each person entering leadership and deny access to men and women who would work out their own personality issues on the unsuspecting body of Christ. It is time to upgrade our ministerial skills. And it is time to implement ministerial supervision for our staffs involved in counseling relationships. People have a right to expect competence, confidentiality, and an open referral to appropriate help when we are clearly out of our areas of expertise.

Some churches will have to face the difficult and painful process of dealing with an individual who has run amok among the flock. But the consequences of not dealing with such a leader are dire

We have used and abused our pulpits and classrooms to deal with private family matters.

Some church members fear that their intimate lives will become material for the minister's Sunday illustration or next big talk. I have seen ministers who are so frustrated with a counseling case, or their own families, that they design whole sermons to address that one person or family. This is a total misuse of positional power and the confidential ministerial relationship. One longtime member of a congregation shared with me, "I can usually tell what's going on between the preacher and his wife." I asked, "How can you tell that?" He replied, "Well, when it comes to the application of his sermon, he normally looks at her and runs through the same agenda he's been trying to convince her of for many years. We have bets on whether his preaching or her stubbornness will hold out the longest."

We should ask permission to use someone's story or testimony. I have on many occasions asked clients who have shared a touching story if I might repeat it publicly. Once again, we must create a private, confidential atmosphere for issues that are intended to be ministered to by the very few.

We have shot our wounded or left them for dead.

Some churches mistreat their wounded marriages and families. Rather than expend the time and energy to haul the wounded back to camp, they would rather let them die a death far removed from the church. The result of such an attitude sends shock waves for generations to come.

We cannot ignore the fact that churches are known for their ministry skills. People in pain talk about the response of the local church. If they are ignored, judged, preached at, or made to be a public spectacle, they will talk. They will assign a reputation to that church as being a museum for the saints, not a hospital for the sinners.

They have seen too much joy in corrective actions in the past.

I recall visiting a church where an announcement was made that someone was no longer a brother in fellowship due to his marital failure. The details of the announcement did not make as big an impact on me as the tone of the announcement maker. He seemed to take some satisfaction in announcing the tragic series of events.

When I read the New Testament, I read about a group of people that had to self-discipline their ranks. Church discipline was clearly a part of the life of the local church. However, in each case that I have studied, the tone was one of sorrow and godly compassion, not joyfulness and retribution.

I discipline my children out of love and sadness. It's never a fun chore to correct my kids. But I know I must so that they may grow in responsibility and wholeness. God treats us as His children. He disciplines us for our growth as Christians. But He doesn't do it out of a desire to get even. He does it out of love. We must approach our relationships in God's larger family with the same unconditional love that He expresses to us. To do less is to miss the entire mission of the New Testament church.

They have seen us standardless in regard to family life.

Our world is hungry for a word from God concerning the family. During my years of teaching family relations, I discovered students were eager to learn what God's Word had to say about their everyday struggles. They were amazed that the Bible was so relevant.

We can hold up a standard. We can hold up the ideal of monogamous marriage. We can hold up the expectations for reasonable child care and protection. We can speak of the pain of addiction and excesses. We can speak of the sanctity of human life.

We can do all of this while ministering to divorced persons, pregnant teenagers, addicted businesspeople, and homeless people. It is not a compromise of the gospel to hold up the ideal and to minister where people have suffered and failed.

Jesus said, "Those who are well have no need of a physician, but those who are sick" (Luke 5:31). He made it clear that He had come "to preach the gospel to the poor" (Luke 4:18).

The barriers may seem substantial. In many cases they are. However, the good news is, many congregations will respond quickly and authentically to a family life ministry that seeks to meet human needs from God's Word. It does not take long for people to learn that this ministry is different. People think, *This ministry is really concerned about my struggles and the struggles of my friends. This is a place where I could really use my gifts and talents.*

Overcoming Institutional Barriers

I refer to the barriers in this chapter as institutional ones because they tend to be a part of the unwritten rules of the entire church family. As the family life minister, you may face a long process of addressing these issues. With patience and an ongoing attempt to create a healthy family atmosphere, you can help the church re-create a more effective response to family life. Here are some general suggestions:

- Help the local church define family ministry in broader terms than counseling or a counseling center.
- Help church leaders make friends with counseling and psychology. Lead them in a study of the integration of psychology and theology, and assist in the demystification process of therapy.
- Affirm all life crises as worthy of legitimate ministry.
- Assist church leaders in defining *success* as both qualitative and quantitative. Emphasize edification and evangelism as necessary for balanced church growth.
- Help build staff relations and expertise.
- Assist in training leaders and members as encouragers and people helpers.

- Assist as a congregational healer in conditions of congregational conflict.
- Explore prejudices against groups of persons.
- Avoid supplying simplistic answers to complex problems.
- Teach out of your struggles as well as your strengths.
- Be open to legitimate censure and supervision, and encourage openness among all ministers.
- Model acceptance of people with "unacceptable" struggles.
- Expose denial by insisting that church leaders listen and understand the nature of problems among members.
- Keep all confidences, and insist on an unbending standard of privacy and professionalism. Short-circuit congregational grapevines and information chains.
- Model vulnerability and transparency with the members and the leaders.

Conclusion

When I first began my ministry in family life, I was not prepared for the presence and intensity of barriers to ministering with families. I supposed that all God's people understood the necessity of ministering with grace to points of pain. That was not the case.

We have made great strides in addressing many of the barriers to family ministry in the local church. But many of these barriers still exist—and will for years to come. The response to this situation is not to throw up our hands in despair and declare the situation hopeless. Nor is the answer to run headlong into the teeth of a shark just to prove it will attack.

The answer is to raise up a generation of compassionate, wise people who will slowly and doggedly turn the ship of the local church back into the winds of change. These family life ministers will carry on their shoulders the weight of concern for church, community, and ministerial families. They will experience defeat time and time again at the hands of congregational fears, prejudices, and pride.

But in time they will help the local church experience the pain and thrill that come when we walk with our families "through the valley of the shadow of death" and arrive by God's grace better off than we were when we started.

May God raise up a generation of people dedicated to all Christian families!

4

PROGRAMMING TO MEET FELT NEEDS

Walking through the church building was like touring pre–World War I Europe. The various ministries looked like a loose coalition of countries on the brink of war just waiting for someone to cross over the wrong boundary at the wrong time.

Claims to classrooms and other important territory had been laid years earlier. Bulletin boards, communication pieces, and congregational recruitment not so subtly proclaimed, "It's our ministry against them, so join up with us!" The main traffic areas and foyers were uncared for no-man's-lands in the congregational landscape.

"What programs do you have going on here?" I asked.

"Programs. We've got programs running out our ears. Programs here and programs there. They all want more money, more push from the pulpit, more and better trained volunteers. But what's driving me crazy is the incessant turf battles and unwillingness of any ministry leader to look at how well the ministry is accomplishing its goals. We are busy, but I'm not sure anything is really happening," replied the minister.

"We seem to be growing like an unkempt backyard. Just ignore the weeds so long as there is some grass growing out there. Keep the yard mowed real short and maybe the neighbors won't notice. I just wish we could stop and take a good look at our programs to see if they are helping people or if our people exist to serve them!" he continued.

"So what's your plan?" I inquired.

"It depends on what day you ask me," he said. "There's a part of me that would like to chuck all the programs entirely and get out with people every day and react to whatever God opens up in front of me."

Say the word *programs* and see the hair on the back of people's necks stand up. Programs have often been labeled as the problem in church work. Sometimes they are! Like my minister friend, we want to flush the entire system down the drain and try to start over from scratch.

But activities and ministries should be the end result of a programming process that leads to implementing effective ministries. If done correctly, a programming process helps us identify felt needs, evaluate options to meet the needs, implement programs that target the needs, and evaluate progress so no program becomes a sacred cow.

Unfortunately, too many times in local work we get sidetracked by the urgent and forget the important. We rarely have the luxury of getting above the daily grind and looking at the entire landscape. The processes discussed in this chapter are useful in establishing a family life ministry. The programming process is equally valid for any ministry that wants to set goals based on needs and a prioritized approach. Given the high level of waste of human, monetary, and time resources in most churches, I view a programming model as good stewardship of God's gifts.

Programming Defined

Programming is an ongoing process. Programming has been described as *a rational-purposive process designed to access, address, and evaluate the needs of a system with the overall goal of effecting a desired change.*

As you can see from the definition, we are dealing with many different theories of human interaction and change. Programming will use concepts of need theory, decision making, statistics, organizational communications, power, and planning. These elements exist and are dynamic factors in every local church to some degree. Each family minister must learn to understand their impact on the ministry.

Programming includes several phases: planning, developing, implementing, monitoring, and evaluating. The process of programming differs from one phase to another as I will describe in this chapter.

Programming and Planned Change

Through programming, changes occur at a structural and functional level of church life. It involves definition—the creation of new ideas; diffusion—the communication of new ideas; decision—the adoption or rejection of new ideas; and consequences—the effects of new ideas.

Change may be rapid or slow, orderly or haphazard. The most effective family ministry implements a change process that is rapid enough to address the needs of the church and community while moving slowly enough to acquaint the church with the need for the new ministry.

A church considered implementing a premarital counseling program. As the staff discussed the idea, everyone agreed that couples needed to participate in several sessions before heading to the altar.

Then came the rub: Are we going to require this of our members? Will we allow a couple to schedule a wedding without completing this requirement? How will we make the transition into this new policy? What if couples refuse to participate? These are all programming questions that deal with planned change. Unless we manage the change process, we will be unable to implement any new idea in the church.

You must manage change effectively to create a family environment within the church system. Change that is implemented in a thoughtless or haphazard way opens the door for rejection of additional ideas or the entire ministry later on. You must read the pulse of the church to implement ministry programs that target felt needs and address them in a way that is palatable to the church.

Conditions Necessary for Successful Change

Since family ministry is usually a new endeavor for a local church, many leaders ask how they can effectively implement change in an existing church system. How can you approach the change process to assure a more favorable acceptance of the new ministry? The conditions must be set for successful change to be implemented:

1. Members and leaders must believe it is their plan and not totally decided by outsiders.
2. Leaders in the church must support the change.
3. The recommended changes must be reasonable and in line with the stated and unstated values and beliefs of the church members.
4. Members and leaders should experience support in the change process.
5. Members and leaders should feel their security and autonomy are not threatened.

If these conditions can be set and maintained, the family ministry sets the framework for a mutually supportive relationship among ministry, members, and leaders. Early in a ministry assignment I failed to create a strong relationship with one of the key opinion leaders. He wanted a particular ministry implemented in the counseling center, and I strongly opposed it. In the process of defeating that motion I failed to maintain a supportive relationship with him. The end result was a polarization that was never reversed. The leader never trusted my advice, and the relationship was always strained.

Change is tricky business at best. In family ministry, the management of change is a key factor in determining the effectiveness of the program. In plain terms it boils down to people skills. How effective are you in moving toward the goals and taking other people with you? If you fail at this task, you will have a long uphill climb.

Programming: An Overview of the Conceptual Framework

There are many models of programming. I will suggest a few that have broad applications and are easily used. Most models have five phases:

Phase One: Planning
1. Awareness: What is the need or the problem?
2. Analysis: What do we know of the entire situation?
3. Conclusions: What decisions or possible solutions can we come to?
4. Limitations: What problems can we address? What problems can we not address?

Phase Two: Developing
1. Purposes
2. Goals
3. Objectives
4. Activities
5. Tasks
6. Elements

Phase Three: Implementing
1. Policies
2. Strategies
3. Actions

Phase Four: Monitoring
1. Processes
2. Performances
3. Resources used
4. Activities

Phase Five: Evaluating
1. Purposes: Policy level evaluation
2. Goals: Long-range evaluation
3. Objectives: Short-range evaluation
4. Outcomes
5. Impact

Using these five stages, you can be sure of identifying the needs of the family, implementing programs to meet those needs, and evaluating adequately the results of the programs.

Returning to the example of the church struggling to implement a premarital program, the first task was to develop a comprehensive philosophy that was appropriate to the church and setting. Once the parameters of the program were set and agreed upon, the new premarital program was implemented and field-tested for a period of time. The church decided to require a minimum of four sessions of counseling for each couple before scheduling the wedding on the church calendar. After the new policy was established, the change was communicated in a positive way to the church, and a date was set several months ahead to begin implementing the program. A second date was set six months later to review the effectiveness of the new program and fine-tune it. The ministers moved through all five phases of planning with the program.

The Reality of Programming

Theory in books is great, but in practice can we really implement these five phases? Churches generally do not plan adequately. There are four major areas of discrepancy from the ideal approach to real life.

1. *Inadequate needs analysis.* Research seems to indicate that very little needs assessment is actually done in church work. Reasons for this inattention include lack of time, expertise, and the resources to do an adequate job. In other words, we implement programs without assessing the real need for them first.

2. *Systematic determination of objectives.* Focused objectives should evolve out of the needs analysis. The end result of this analysis should be a prioritized list of the objectives for a ministry or an entire church. Often one person or one small group decides the priorities for a church with little input.

3. *Designing instruction.* Very little attention is given to using the body of knowledge pertaining to instructional design in the educational efforts of the local church. Pressure to bring programs on line quickly results in classes, seminars, and groups that use ineffective approaches with adult learners.

4. *Comprehensive evaluation.* Most churches do little evaluation of any programs or ministries. Like our illustration in the beginning of

this chapter, programs take on lives of their own and often become the focus of the church rather than tools for doing good. Educational programs are offered with no attention to follow-up and evaluation of the curriculum, teacher, or methodology.

Growing churches are rapidly learning the truth of the adage that "less is often more." The family ministry would do well to offer a few high-quality programs that flow out of a systematic process of planning.

At this point let's examine briefly the phases of programming and how they affect the development of the family life ministry.

Needs Analysis and Its Importance

Needs analysis is so important that I have devoted an entire chapter to it. It is the starting point in the process of developing family ministry. It defines "what is" in contrast to "what ought to be." But needs analysis goes beyond the identification process to help you prioritize needs and the allocation of scarce resources.

A word of caution is in order. Churches often articulate the deep desire to be felt-need driven. Many do an excellent job of fulfilling that dream. However, the reality of church life dictates that it is often not the congregational or community needs that dictate the direction of the ministry. The values, beliefs, and personality of the church or religious body as a whole define the kind of family ministry that can be developed and, most important, the form of ministry that cannot be developed.

The family ministry that blindly expects a mere identification of needs to immediately stir the church to unified action is setting the stage for disappointment. Many church leaders look at the needs of families and refuse or deny their existence. In the more extreme examples, they assassinate the messengers. Information is a powerful tool in the change process and must be managed effectively.

Where do you get information for a needs analysis? Information should come from many sources, including existing records of what has been done, interviews, surveys, existing literature, direct observation, inquiry, files and records of staff, and informal analysis.

After you have gathered the necessary information, what next? What do you do with all of the data? That depends on how you answer several questions:

- What information do we now have?
- How does it match what we are currently doing?
- Does it match our expectations?
- What of it is related to our vision?
- What of it is related to our goals?
- Of all the things we could do now, what should we do?
- If we could do only one thing, what would it be?

Figure 4.1 illustrates how needs analysis is the beginning point for a programming model. Notice that it is directly related to goals and the use of resources.

Setting Program Goals

Once you have determined the needs of the group you are trying to reach, you can think about the goals and the major areas you need to address.

Goals in family ministry should be characterized by the following traits: a long-range time frame, broad areas of emphasis versus specific target activities, and the ability to be measured for achievement.

For example, I conducted a series of surveys with three thousand Christian families worshiping in urban churches larger than one

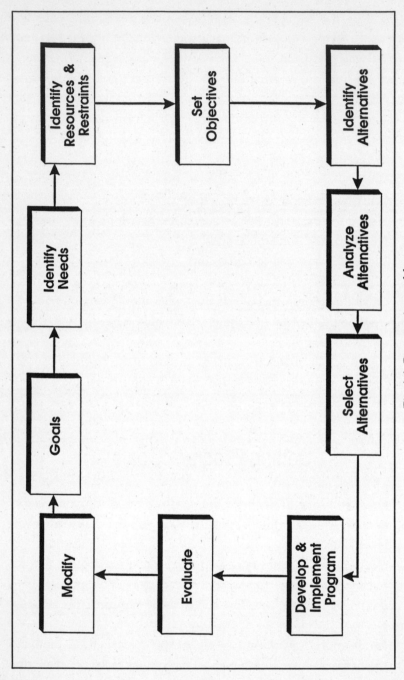

Fig. 4.1 Programming model

thousand members using the instrument included in the Appendix. It revealed a pattern of ministry needs. When the needs were translated into goals, the following statements were drafted:

Goal 1: To address the spiritual needs of the families in terms of individual, couple, and family spiritual development.

Goal 2: To address the stresses on marriages at all stages of the marital life cycle.

Goal 3: To assist parents of young children and teens to learn effective communications, problem solving, and discipline, and to build self-esteem.

Goal 4: To assist the aging population and those responsible for their care.

Goal 5: To help Christian families select recreational and entertainment options that build family unity and values.

Goal 6: To assist Christian singles and couples in building relationships outside the family network.

Goal 7: To help develop family, church, and community leadership skills within the members of the family.

These goals provided a framework for developing a comprehensive training model that kept the ministry busy for several years. That training model was illustrated with a pyramid to underscore the priorities that each need area dictated (see fig. 4.2).

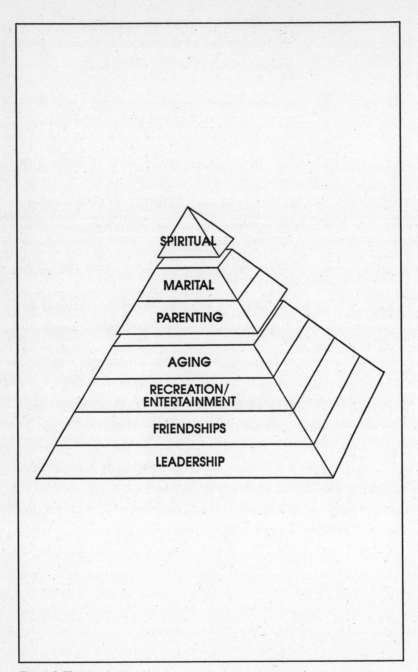

Fig. 4.2. Training issues

Setting Program Objectives

After identifying goals, you are ready to address ministry objectives. Some leaders simply move from the data to setting short-term objectives. I have seen them read one survey or react to one conversation and immediately throw time, money, and staff resources at the problem. This reactive method of planning and programming leads to a fire drill mentality among the staff. Ultimately, leaders, ministers, and members become frustrated because of the lack of organization and focus of the ministry.

You must assist the church in implementing this programming approach in the ministry. Your role would include the following tasks:

- Help leaders forge an appropriate mission statement for the ministry.
- Assist in generating purpose and goal statements.
- Set, along with family ministry leaders, program objectives.
- Serve as a resource person as ministry leaders set subobjectives.
- Support and provide resources for the achievement of all tasks and action steps.
- Monitor all processes of each level of operation, and facilitate the communication system.

How does this translate into actual practice? How do needs turn into goal statements with the appropriate objectives? Consider the example of needs data used to generate compatible objectives and goals (see fig. 4.3). The illustration is based upon a church that has just conducted a needs analysis. The data indicate a high incidence of divorce in the church and strain on marital relationships in general.

Need Statement:	Married couples in this church are divorcing and in need of our help.
Goal Statement:	To assist people who are divorcing or considering it as an option.

Policy Level		**Goal Hierarchy**	
Need 1	Counseling for them	Goal 1	To counsel
Need 2	Social support networks	Goal 2	To give support
Need 3	Preventive programs	Goal 3	To teach and train

Objectives Level

Objective 1:   Counseling and referral services
Objective 2:   Divorce group
Objective 3:   Marriage enrichment program

Subobjectives

Subobjective 1:   Dialogue with area counselors
Subobjective 2:   Train a group leader
Subobjective 3:   Hold a marriage enrichment seminar

Fig. 4.3. Needs data

As figure 4.3 illustrates, goals become objectives the farther down the hierarchy you go. Goals are typically long range, more general, and strategically oriented. Objectives tend to be short range, more specific, and tactical.

Program Evaluation

In Genesis, Lot was challenged to find fewer and fewer righteous souls in Sodom. Fewer and fewer ministers take the time to ask, Is what I am so busily engaged in accomplishing my goals?

Evaluation means more than passing out a one-page survey at the end of a class or seminar. It is more than phoning a couple of members and asking them if they enjoyed the meeting. Proper program evaluation is an ongoing process that should affect every area of planning. It involves three key functions: (1) ascertaining the decision areas of concern in a program; (2) selecting the appropriate information needed in the decision-making process; and (3) collecting and analyzing information to report summary material useful in decision making.

Effective evaluation has many dynamic characteristics. It is a process that uses many strategies; it is a management tool; it is a people-centered activity. Effective evaluation accounts for past activities, present activities, and future commitments.

Evaluation may take two forms in church work. *Summative evaluation* is conducted for the purpose of justifying or accounting for program and institutional involvements. It is usually conducted by an external agent. It is useful when the church or ministry is experiencing problems, has stalled at a level of growth, or has ceased to achieve its major goals. Leaders typically call for summative evaluation after they have exhausted all internal resources in dealing with the issues confronting them.

The most common form of evaluation in family ministry is *formative evaluation*. Formative evaluation is conducted for the purpose of improving programs. It seeks to gain information on the program during the delivery phase in order to remedy any shortcomings. It is useful for a multitude of planning purposes.

Tools of formative evaluation may include the following:

- Written response forms and surveys
- Structured interviews
- Open interviews
- Input from key leaders and facilitators
- Informal conversation
- Written follow-up or testing
- Participant comparison to other programs

Evaluation information is useful to you in several ways. It helps you evaluate how the target audience perceived the program. It helps evaluate how well you are meeting goals and objectives. It serves as a reference point when leaders question the budget or the use of volunteers in a ministry. Opinions from the minister are valid, but a ministry that constantly monitors its effectiveness will go a long way in building the trust and respect of the congregation and the leaders.

As our church developed a family ministry that was both inreach and outreach oriented, our family ministry committee was forced to rethink what success would look like in the ministry. After a great deal of discussion, we determined that our effectiveness would be multidimensional and would produce at least seven results:

1. The deepening of the overall quality of Christian family life
2. The restoration of members who are marginally involved with the life of the local church due to some family crisis
3. A growing body of searchers who are not members of the local church but increasing in their relationship with and dependence upon the body of Christ as a real agent in their lives

4. Higher congregational usage of and involvement in the family life ministry
5. A growing number of referrals and contacts who are involved in family ministry offerings
6. The teaching and conversion of searchers to the body of Christ
7. An image in the local community that sees the church as a positive, proactive force for families of all types

Summary

I have proposed a model of programming in this chapter that moves from identifying felt needs to setting goals, objectives, and tasks. The importance of evaluation in every area of the ministry builds a foundation for trust and helps focus the ministry on the future as well as the present. The family minister must learn to be a trusted change agent in the church. Programming is vital when a new ministry is being launched. It helps the church choose from among the many needs that are expressed in the congregation and community.

In the next chapter we will focus on one specific area of programming. Needs analysis is the beginning point in the programming model because it defines the felt needs.

5

CONDUCTING A CONGREGATIONAL FAMILY NEEDS ANALYSIS

I had been called in to consult with a large urban church in a growing metropolitan area. The minister assured me on the phone that the leaders were anxious to learn how they could effectively minister to their families.

"What should we do first?" he asked.

I suggested a congregational family needs analysis.

"Sounds ominous. What's that?"

"It's just an X ray of the condition of your families right now."

"Great, my guys will be in favor of that. These management types love to see the numbers, you know!"

I tried in vain to explain that it involved a lot more than passing out another survey. Several hundred work hours later I stood in the conference room and began to unveil the results.

"Gentlemen, we surveyed your congregation during the Bible class hour. Here we found that almost 50 percent of the adult population in your Bible classes reported a need for individual, marital, and family counseling."

The room became very still. Not a word was spoken. Eyes hit the table as I finished the report. An hour later I asked, "Does anyone have any questions?" Not a man spoke. "Could I give you any more information about the children, the singles, or the married couples?" Not a creature was stirring—not even a mouse!

"Well, how can I help you respond to the needs of these families?"

After a long silence one man spoke up, "Dr. Don, we appreciate your coming all this way to work with us. But right now let's not say anything more about this, shall we?"

On Monday morning it was business as usual, and another report was filed in another nondescript filing cabinet for the church historian to find.

Needs Analysis

Anyone who has been involved with local church work and has the slightest appreciation for the management of human resources cannot help being disturbed by the monumental waste of resources. It is discouraging to see the tremendous waste of time, money, and people due primarily to a lack of effective planning.

The needs of families in our churches and communities are far too great to be ineffective in meeting them. Most churches do not have the luxury to throw people and dollars at ministerial hunches. Since we do not have the ability, as Luke said of Jesus, to "know the hearts of all" (Acts 1:24), we must rely on more mundane methodologies.

Congregational family needs analysis is one of the tools in our tool kit. It is a multifaceted effort to determine what is going on in our congregational families. It allows us to focus our attention on meeting real human needs.

Jesus was constantly barraged with many human needs. He had

to pick and choose from among many competing needs. We must do something similar. We must learn to listen to our churches and communities. We must overcome the temptation to assume we have all the answers and know exactly what is going on within our churches without asking. We must be willing to shape a flexible ministry that begins where our people are suffering, not where our interests lie.

This chapter details the process of conducting a family needs analysis. A sample questionnaire I use in congregational family needs analysis is provided for you in the Appendix. It is an adaptation from Dr. Royce Money's instrument in *Ministering to Families: A Positive Plan of Action*. I have successfully used several variations of this instrument. It will give you some insight into how you can use statistics to generate a report and an overall plan for ministry.

As you move into the nuts and bolts of family ministry, please remember that it is a way of thinking about ministry. It is a new philosophy of ministry that deals with the individual, couple, and family in a holistic way. You must not get lost in the details of planning and forget the overall goals of the ministry.

What Is a Needs Analysis?

A Needs Identification Process

Most church leaders think they have an excellent idea of what the members think and feel. Some leaders do. Many do not. Ministers and church leaders may hear regularly from a select number of people in the congregation. This input gives them a limited view of the church.

Needs analysis allows the leaders to look at the big picture. Large segments of the church may not be effectively ministered to because leaders have not identified they are there! Needs analysis also keeps church leaders from operating in an informational vacuum or suffering from a case of information lag.

A Dream-Inducing Process

As the needs of the church surface, you will see new possibilities for family life ministry. New dreams and visions may take shape as the leaders discuss how to effectively meet the needs.

This process may also open the door for the entire church to evaluate the present dream: Have we accomplished all we set out to accomplish? Do we have any direction at all? Often, when one ministry launches out with aggressive dreams, the whole church will step up the pace.

A Needs Prioritization Process

Needs analysis not only discovers needs but also addresses which needs are most important.

In the illustration at the beginning of the chapter, the church had many congregational needs. The most glaring one was the stress already present in the families. The immediate need was for counseling and referrals. Other preventive programs needed to be addressed, but they would have to take a back seat for the moment.

A Strategy-Focusing Process

Needs analysis focuses energy and effort. It helps prioritize your time, the development of programs, and the use of human resources. By setting immediate and long-term goals, the ministry can prioritize strategies that will meet the needs of the church.

A Resource Direction Process

Directing the resources of time, money, and people is crucial in large and small congregations. Smaller churches may have more limited budgets and be concerned with getting the most from every dollar spent. Larger churches, faced with an overwhelming number of congregational needs, may be confused as to which are the most pressing. Needs analysis helps you direct your resources to the points of pain.

What Type of Planning Is Used Currently?

My involvement with churches has revealed at least six approaches to identifying and meeting the needs of families. Some of these approaches depend on the wisdom and insight of one person, usually the minister. These approaches are the most dangerous. Only two, the life cycle approach and the customized approach, provide you with valid results.

The Special Emphasis Approach

Using this approach, the minister carves out two or three Sundays per year to address the needs of the family. These sermons, normally preached on Mother's Day and Father's Day, apply a thick coating of guilt to the audience. A call to traditional home life is leveled with no acknowledgment of current struggles. Courageous attempts by members to build strong Christian families in the face of an alien culture are ignored. Members leave the church believing the minister has no understanding of their daily struggles.

The Ready, Fire, Aim Approach

Some churches, like people, are in a hurry to do something! Churches of this type suffer from two problems. First, they neglect to take aim. Focus is extremely important in family ministry where the needs are so great and usually the resources are limited. Second, they may rely on an inaccurate scout. They mount up and ride off in the wrong direction because they are operating from inaccurate information.

The Shotgun Approach

Some churches are blessed with the financial resources to throw money at problems. Others see a need and are quick to assign it to a staff person, who may or may not be equipped to handle the problems. Some quickly develop a program, initiate it, and then drop it within two years.

The shotgun approach fails to take aim. Like the ready, fire, aim approach, it is not interested in the target. These churches load up and assume if they put enough shot in the sanctuary, they are bound to hit something. Unfortunately, it is often failure.

The Latest Film, Topic, or Speaker Approach

Some churches like to play the "greatest hits" game. Whatever the latest film series, the hottest topic, the most interesting speaker or seminar—they want to be the first to offer it to their people. Never mind if the topic or speaker is relevant to their people. They did something! This is really not family ministry; it is seminar ministry.

The key question in family ministry continues to be, Have we effected any change in the lives of our families based on the ministry? Churches with "the latest" approach seldom slow down to answer that question—they are off listening to the latest hot topic.

The Life Cycle Approach

This approach is a valid method of analyzing congregational needs without going through the steps outlined in the remainder of this chapter. Essentially, you do a head count of the ages in the church. You divide them by marital types: singles, young couples, young families, and so on. Then you graph each age and marital type on a chart to determine how many folks are in each developmental stage.

Needs may be projected by consulting any life cycle or family developmental textbook. This method is far from being foolproof, but it is a way to get an estimate of where the church may need help. I do not recommend this method as a substitute for a more comprehensive analysis, but it can be helpful when general data are needed in a short period of time.

The Customized Approach

I recommend the customized approach to family needs analysis because it is the most comprehensive and flexible. It allows you the luxury of shaping the study to fit your church and gives an in-depth picture of the entire congregation. Once the analysis is completed, you and the leaders will have a healthy grasp on the condition of church families. The customized approach takes some time, but the time spent in identifying needs will pay big dividends in directly ministering to felt needs.

A church located in an older urban area conducted a comprehensive family needs analysis with its members. The results of the study showed that there were many widows and retired adults with special needs that were not being addressed. When it was time to evaluate staffing needs, the leaders opted for a minister to mature adults instead of a replacement for the youth minister who was working with a small segment of the church. The needs analysis allowed the church to identify and prioritize its most pressing family concerns.

What Are the Characteristics of an Effective Needs Analysis?

An Unbiased, Open Process

A valid needs analysis is free from the bias of one person or group in the church. It presents the data without a slant toward anyone's particular agenda. It is open to complete investigation by leaders and members.

Leaders may survey members to validate preconceived conclusions. One church took a yearly missions survey. The members were asked to rank their preferences in mission points. The committee had a vested interest in foreign missions, but each year the church ranked stateside involvements at the top of the list. When 60 percent of the church called for greater local mission efforts, the committee reported, "An impressive 40 percent of this church is committed to our foreign missions program as it now stands."

A survey of this nature teaches church members negative lessons. It teaches them the process is biased and closed. It teaches them that their opinion doesn't really mean anything. Finally, it teaches them not to be involved. I have found that an open, honest needs analysis can be a breath of fresh air to some church members.

A Multidimensional Process

Needs analysis is a multidimensional process that involves the collection and analysis of many types of information. The final report and plan should reflect input from many sources outside the survey instrument.

I caution you strongly against reprinting the survey in this book, making five hundred copies, and distributing them to the unsuspecting congregation. Needs analysis requires time and preparation to be successful. When our ministry begins this process, it usually requires a minimum of six months from start to finish. During this time, we prepare the church, talk with the people, survey, analyze, and follow a goal-setting process. Take your time and take the church along with you in the process.

A Recurring Process

Needs analysis is never ending. The goal is to replicate the analysis every twenty-four to thirty-six months. You may assume you will spend all of your time in a closed room with stacks of surveys. Certainly not!

Family ministry must have a constant flow of information feedback from the church. This is important for two reasons. First, many churches will change significantly in membership in two or three years. You need to touch base to see what changes have occurred since the last time you surveyed. Second, a needs analysis gives you feedback into the effectiveness of the program.

If a church said they were struggling with teaching Christian values in the home as a top training need two years ago, the next analysis should show some improvement in this situation if the ministry has been targeted correctly. If it remains high as a need, you should ask some additional questions.

A Broad-Based Process

An effective family needs analysis should include every group within the church. It should give fair and unbiased attention to every age group and marital status within the congregation, regardless of size. It should not be used as a tool for one ministry to promote growth over another ministry. It should not be used by one individual within the congregation to promote a particular special interest or hobby. By making the family needs analysis a broad-based activity, you will help build consensus within the congregation for the needs of the entire church family.

An Anonymous Process

One of the most common questions church leaders ask concerning family needs analysis is related to the confidentiality of the survey. Most leaders are worried that we will survey very sensitive areas within the church and then use that information to identify members later on. A needs analysis process should be anonymous.

Complete confidentiality should be promised and maintained throughout the entire project. Only people who are trustworthy and skilled in the handling of sensitive information should work on the project and in the family ministry itself.

A Personal and Dynamic Process for Leaders

I have made the point that family ministry may unearth unresolved issues at the core of the leadership. This may begin to surface during the family needs analysis process. Typically, a church leader or minister who is hesitant to learn more about the struggles of the congregation will be the same individual who is suffering within the family.

The needs analysis may also define differences in ministry style among the church staff. As serious family issues are discussed, ministers and church leaders may discover that they have radically different approaches to meeting those needs. It is much better that those differences be laid on the table and discussed than to remain hidden.

A Process That Leads to Focus

I have said repeatedly that family ministry must be focused and planned. The needs analysis is the first step in moving toward that goal. As you identify new and varied needs within the church, the staff may begin to evaluate the effectiveness of other ministries within the church. If the church has been in existence for a long period of time, some ministries may be functioning without a real goal. Others may have ceased to be usable when compared to current needs. Still others may need redefining and redesigning. Many churches find this process—known as cutting the alligator's tail—to be extremely painful. It is never easy to initiate organizational change, especially within the church. However, the needs analysis can give you a basis for evaluating ministries in light of actual congregational data.

A Process That Leads to Integration of Many Ministries

An effective analysis provides information on many areas of ministries. For the education minister, it can be a basis for curriculum analysis. For the pulpit minister, it can provide audience analysis in the preparation and delivery of sermons. The youth minister can get keen insight into the lives of teenagers. Day care directors can plan for the development and expansion of preschool and nursery programs. Involvement ministries can see opportunities to use members in ways that have never been anticipated before. Church leaders can gain information concerning areas of shepherding, counseling, and pastoral care. The effective family minister will compose the report and plan of action with an eye toward assisting other staff ministers and ministry leaders in applying the data to their areas of interest.

Family Needs Analysis: A Step-by-Step Procedure

At this point we begin a description of a step-by-step procedure to complete a comprehensive family needs analysis in a local church. There are ten major steps that you must follow.

Step 1: Obtaining Leaders' Agreement on the Project's Viability

As the illustration at the beginning of the chapter documented, producing a family needs analysis is no guarantee that any action will follow. It is crucial for you, the family life minister, to understand that unless you have the agreement of the leaders of the church for the completion of the needs analysis, a plan of action will not likely be implemented in the church. It is risky business to produce a needs analysis in hopes that it will convince hesitant or stubborn leaders. More often, the report is dismissed, and the church goes back to business as usual.

Spend time discussing the family needs analysis project with all church leaders. Explain the goals of the needs analysis to them individually, and allow them to ask questions in private. This approach will provide an opportunity for dialogue and will build consensus for the project. It will also allow the leaders to ask some of the more critical questions in a nonthreatening environment.

If you are able to secure leaders' commitment toward the needs analysis, you can be sure that they will be more likely to participate willingly and go to the congregation with more enthusiasm. It is a powerful sight to see united leaders and church staff standing before a congregation committing itself to meeting the needs of the church family and the needs of the families in the neighborhood. Properly done, a needs analysis can bring this kind of consensus to the leaders of the church. Improperly done, it can cause divisions among the leaders and the staff that will be very difficult to repair.

I have seen congregations that are not quite ready to launch into a needs analysis process. Even though the pain is present in the congregation, the leaders may not be ready to hear. The denial mechanisms may be too strong. It may take a few more months or a few more years for the pain to reach into the hearts of the leaders. At other times, it may require a few cases that strike very close to the core of the church to go public. In any case, I see churches moving toward the recognition of family problems and a more adequate response.

Step 2: Assembling the Analysis Team

A ministry team should conduct the family needs analysis. Members of the team should be highly committed to the family life ministry. They should have some background in planning, research design, statistics, or information processes if possible. They should reflect the broad-based membership of the congregation at large. They should be trained to deal with confidential information. Often, a needs analysis will surface many other issues within the church family that have remained unspoken for many years. These individuals should be capable of handling such information without passing it on to the rest of the church family.

There is a temptation to approach the needs analysis with only one person. Although it may seem more efficient, it can be dangerous. We conducted a needs analysis for a congregation where 80 percent of the young people were under the age of ten. When the youth minister was presented the report, he looked at the pie chart and remarked, "Look at all the teenagers in this church. It looks like I'm going to have to go for a bigger budget!" His response dramatically illustrates the need for more than one person to interpret the data. We all come to the analysis process with biases. In the development of the family ministry a group of trained and competent individuals must look at the X ray of the church and then make some general conclusions free from individual interests.

An analysis team for a congregation of six hundred might include the family minister and four or five other individuals within the congregation. Typically, these individuals will be members of the family ministry committee, although that is not always the case. At times, the elders will request a representative on the analysis team, although that is not essential. The analysis team should be presented to the congregation, charged with the task of ministering to the felt needs of the families. They may be involved with every stage of the process, although usually one person, the family life minister, writes the final report.

Step 3: Projecting a Reasonable Timetable

The analysis team should set aside a reasonable amount of time for the needs analysis. Larger congregations (one thousand members or more) may require as long as four to six months. Medium and smaller churches may require less time. Much of this time is spent preparing the church and leaders, analyzing the data, and preparing a ministry plan of action.

The analysis team should prepare a projected timetable and present it to the leaders. Care should be taken to try to abide by the projected dates, especially once the formal survey has been conducted. Many congregations become survey weary and feel nothing will be done with their information. Our team typically promises to read each survey written the afternoon following the administration of the survey.

Step 4: Communicating the Intent to Do Strategic Planning

The analysis team should advise the leaders and the congregation of the intent to do strategic planning. Many people will ask skeptically, "Why do we need to give you information about our family?" A concerned reply that communicates the family ministry's interest in all families of the church and an assurance that the information will be kept confidential are helpful.

You or the chairperson of the analysis team should periodically update the congregation on the status of the project. The members should be informed repeatedly concerning the purpose of the project. An announcement or a letter that promises a full report on a Sunday morning may go a long way to build cooperation among church members.

Step 5: Determining the Information Desired

The analysis team will need to discuss what information they want to gather, both formally and informally. The typical survey I have used gathers information on these crucial areas of family concern:

- Demographics: What can we discover about age, sex, marital status, education, occupation, hours worked, and so on?
- Areas of training: In what areas do we need to offer preventive training to our families?
- Areas of need: What areas are already demanding attention by the family ministry?
- Delivery: How can we best tailor our preventive and therapeutic programs to meet the schedules of our people?

These areas are the heart of the survey instrument. The analysis team will need to address many other questions in addition to the formal survey. These questions will be unique to the individual congregation but might include the following:

- What is currently being done for families?
- What has been done in the past?
- Where do our families go for help?
- What resources exist in our community to help?
- Who in the church is being overlooked in ministry?
- How do we treat singles, couples, and families that are having problems?
- Which families in the church are doing an exemplary job? Why?
- Which families in the church have had a difficult time? Why?
- Are there any common denominators in the families that are doing well?
- Are there any common denominators in the families that are struggling?
- What do the leaders say about family life in this church?
- What do the ministers say about family life in this church?
- Who are the fringe members and fringe families in this church, and why are they there?

This is just a partial list of the questions an analysis team might ask in exploring the world of families in the church. Each team will generate a list; each analysis will be different. Questions for informal review should be generated before and after the survey. For instance, if people over the age of sixty fail to check any area of family interest, does it mean they are negative to the ministry, or does the survey fail to hit upon any of their felt needs? This question could be answered only by a follow-up conversation with some members of that age group.

As the family life minister, you will need to keep the process moving. The survey will generate information and ideas that could stall the analysis team in analysis paralysis.

Step 6: Determining the Methods to Secure the Information

Many methods are available to you as you try to understand the nature and function of the congregational families. I strongly urge you and the analysis team to use a variety of approaches in the needs analysis program. Each method employed will uncover new information. Each road taken will cast new light toward an understanding of the families in the church. Using only a paper and pencil survey will severely limit the understanding of families.

The Congregational Survey This is the most common approach and an indispensable tool for the family ministry. It allows the analysis team to get a broad understanding of the entire congregation. It also provides one-on-one feedback that team members can read. It provides the greatest amount of information in the shortest amount of time. For these reasons, the bulk of the remainder of this chapter will focus on surveying in combination with other information-gathering techniques.

Interviews The good researcher will take time to interview personally a cross section of the congregation. These one-on-one interviews are especially helpful following the congregational survey. Data can be explored with individuals and families. Trends can be analyzed. Hypotheses can be examined.

The interviewing process can be very formal with the research team calling in representative samples of the congregation. These members are then asked to respond to a set series of questions generated by the research team ahead of time. Results are shared and integrated into the formal report.

Interviewing can also be conducted on an informal basis. One family minister observed that family needs began to be communicated to him during his own interviewing process. The leaders of the church and the selection committee were so anxious to communicate the needs of the congregation that they spent very little time asking him any of the traditional interview questions. Their observations became a part of the informal analysis that he used to construct a family life ministry for the congregation.

Interviews could be conducted with some of the following groups:

- Staff members
- Church elders and deacons
- Ministry leaders
- Church secretaries
- Area ministers
- New members
- Founding members
- Members who left in the past year
- Past ministers
- Singles
- Teenagers
- Members in retirement care

You would do well to constantly conduct needs analysis interviews. Walk around the church with an antenna up for the sights and sounds of the church. What are people visiting about? Who comes in alone or late? Who has changed appearance radically in the recent past? Who leaves church in tears? What is being talked about? Which family seems to be fading away from the church now?

By answering these questions, you can gain a better understanding of the congregation. Though this information may be harder to quantify, the final report must reflect the statistics and the "feel" of the congregation. That subjective feel can be ascertained only by a minister who walks with the people.

Staff Interviews I list this separately because it is a vital link in the analysis process. Visiting with each staff member concerning the nature of the families in the church is important for two reasons. First, these men and women are involved with pastoring the flock on a daily basis. They know various segments well if they are doing their jobs. They know what crisis affected the church a year ago. They know which trends are growing and which are declining. Staff ministers can confirm or negate many theories about the family in the local church.

A second reason that ministerial input is significant deals with the concept of integration. Because family ministry can have a wide impact, I have seen many ministers threatened by it. It goes to the heart and core of the church very quickly. If the ministerial staff can have a clear voice in the ministry from the very beginning, many battles over turf or philosophy of ministry can be avoided.

I recommend a visit with all staff ministers before the actual survey is taken. Their participation can increase the likelihood of a successful survey. Once the data have been analyzed, they should be informed as a group of the general direction the ministry is taking. Finally, a comprehensive report should be given to the staff before the congregation sees the ministerial plan of action.

Leadership Interviews You should give the leaders of the church special one-on-one attention throughout the needs analysis and planning stages. Their ownership and input are integral to building a ministry to families. Listen carefully as each leader describes both frustrations and dreams for the families of the church. You will get an idea of how they will view the development of the ministry.

I prefer to conduct these interviews following the data analysis of the survey. With some general numbers in hand, I can gently compare the input from the leaders to reality. Dialogue can begin if there are discrepancies in one's view of reality. I find it unfair and unwise to the ministry to unload statistics and plans on unsuspecting leaders in a short two-hour meeting. It is simply more than they can digest. A preinterview can open up the lines of communications both ways and lay the groundwork for everyone to accept the plans for the ministry.

Small Group Discussion You may wish to call together a variety of small groups to interview them about family stress and needs. These groups typically involve a cross section of the congregation. They may be pulled from the Bible classes, fellowship groups, or other small groups. Care should be taken that they represent many groups within the church family.

The analysis team may wish to prepare a list of questions to explore with the groups. Questions should be open-ended and allow for a free-flowing discussion. An overall time limit, perhaps an hour for seven to ten people, should be set. Notes should be made on the conversation. Two analysis team members are usually needed for this work.

Records and Past Studies With the increasing use of church consultants, many churches have valuable past records of surveys and materials that will be very useful to the analysis team. Statistical records of attendance, Bible classes, and other typical data may provide some useful insights into the congregational surveys.

You may want to review past bulletins to get a feel for programs that have dealt with family themes in the past. This reading will also give you a feel for the corporate congregational story.

Many churches do a poor job of maintaining a master file of important documents and studies. Staff ministers and ministry leaders may spend countless hours working on a major project, and three years later no one can find a copy of the report. Someone on staff should be charged with the mission of gathering and maintaining a historical file of all important studies and reports. The church and the staff can save time and money by avoiding duplicated efforts.

Observation The best analysis team is composed of people watchers. Time spent sitting in the nursery watching the parents drop off the babies, drinking coffee with the retired folks, or teaching in the youth program will give excellent insights into the life of the church. A great deal can be learned by informally watching church members each Sunday.

Imagine yourself seated in the balcony of your church. Think about what went on in the lives of the people in the past week. Imagine all the events that occurred on the way to church that morning. Who lost a job? Who had another fight? What family is concerned about a sick parent a thousand miles away?

When you watch where people sit, who they talk with, how they come and go from the church parking lot, you get a feel for the families that spend 98 percent of their time in another world away from the church building. You have the job of getting inside their world, not building an artificial one in which to place them.

Outside Agents As previously mentioned, many churches rely on an outside church consultant. I know of very few that do direct family needs analysis consulting at the present time. Many factors studied by church growth consultants are not related to the information needed by the family life minister.

A church should be careful in selecting a consultant to assist with the family needs analysis. The consultant should have a strong background in consulting as well as family life ministry. I prefer to use people who have been in the field and know the practical dynamics of family ministry. References should be checked and a clear working contract should be agreed upon prior to the initiation of any study.

Step 7: Determining Appropriate Ways to Secure the Information

Every church is different. Every situation has a unique comfort zone when it comes to filling out a survey. In a graduate class in family ministry, I assigned a group of twenty-five students to conduct a needs analysis in their home or work congregations. The process was as varied as the congregations. Some churches welcomed the information and the process. Others balked at the idea and relegated it to participation by only one Bible class or small group. The analysis team must be prepared to justify its survey methods to the leaders of the church.

Experience has definitely shown that the needs analysis requires as broad-based participation as can be produced. Leaving out any group opens the door to invalid results. Some of my students have experimented with forms that can be used with high-school students. Perhaps a creative family ministry could generate a useful method for gathering information on the church from teens and even younger children. The more complete and varied the picture of the family, the better the chances of developing a well-rounded ministry plan.

The following methods are possibilities for gathering information pertinent to the needs analysis.

Sunday Worship Service Assembly I strongly recommend the Sunday worship service for gathering survey information. It has many positive benefits that will assist the analysis team:

- It provides the broadest range of information.
- It gathers information from the fringe members who may not come to Bible class or return a mailed survey.
- It sends the message to the church that we are serious about meeting your needs.
- It allows an entire worship service to be built around the family ministry theme.
- It allows the analysis team to prepare the church for the ministry plan.
- It provides an opportunity for everyone to receive the same instructions during the administration of the survey.
- It builds a sense of excitement for the ministry.

The most common reservation concerning family surveying during the Sunday morning worship service has to do with time. When ushers are prepared to distribute the form and all the preparation has been made ahead of time, a congregation of one thousand or more can easily be surveyed in about ten minutes. It helps to expedite this process by following these guidelines:

1. Have the directions printed clearly on the front of the survey form and projected on slides or on an overhead projector.
2. The survey administrator should talk the congregation through each step of the survey.
3. Ushers should have stacks of the surveys subdivided by rows to allow quick distribution.
4. Completed surveys should be passed in as soon as they are finished.
5. Analysis team members should be stationed throughout the auditorium to answer questions and give additional directions.

No matter which data collection method you use, you may want to allow members to pick up a survey and complete it a week or two following the formal data collection Sunday. That way everyone who wants to be involved in the study may do so. This is especially important in urban, mobile churches.

You should reassure the congregation of two things at each stage of the study. First, verify that all information will be kept strictly confidential. There is no need for people to sign the survey forms. Second, assure the congregation that you will personally review each form and read every comment.

Bible Class Administration I have used the Bible class hour to administer a needs analysis when the leaders were uncomfortable with a worship assembly administration. But there are drawbacks: it misses fringe members; it biases the statistics to the more involved members of the church; and it lessens the impact of the importance of the family ministry before the whole church.

There are some benefits to using the Bible class hour, however: members generally have more time to complete the survey; it is a more casual atmosphere for administration; and questions can be handled personally by the survey administrator.

Members of the analysis team may be assigned to administer the survey to a class or group. You will need to author instructions for each survey proctor to ensure every class is given the same instructions. It is also a good idea for you to float through the rooms during the administration to answer questions or handle problems.

Mailed Surveys I have never relied on mailed questionnaires for the needs analysis survey. Mailed surveys run the risk of being lost in the junk mail shuffle. A ministry would need to be prepared to make multiple mailings to gain enough data to make the sample statistically meaningful. Mailed surveys might be a useful tool to directly access a smaller group within the church, such as single parents, to do more specific needs assessment. Although mailed surveys offer some real benefits, such as time and anonymity in completion, they present some administrative headaches that the analysis team would need to think through carefully.

Stratified Proportional Random Sampling For the analysis team and family minister with some background in surveys and statistics, this method offers a quicker way to access the trends in the church without dealing with large numbers of surveys.

It is statistically possible and accurate to survey equal segments of the church (proportional strata) without asking each person in that group for input. These samples must be randomly selected using a table of random numbers. The results of this sampling method, if done correctly, should match the results of a survey of all members of the group.

Care should be taken before using this technique. There are many intangible benefits from surveying the entire congregation. The research design of this technique would need to be carefully constructed and carried out. It might save some time in the generation of the data from the surveys, but the interest lost on the part of the entire church being involved would need to be carefully weighed. This technique would be an excellent follow-up tool to a comprehensive survey.

Interviews If you are working with a smaller congregation, or if the analysis team has the luxury of taking its time in preparing a ministry plan of action, the entire needs analysis could be conducted in an interview format. A combination approach might survey demographically each small group participant and then progress into a personal interview concerning training and areas of service needed by the family. For most, the pressure to move through the planning stages to the actual delivery of the ministry program will necessitate a quicker method of assembling the data.

Step 8: Administering and Implementing the Process

At this point you need to review the key points in carrying off a valid needs analysis:

- Have we selected a project chairperson who can see the big picture?
- Have we identified a project writer who can articulate the report in a meaningful, nontechnical manner?
- Are we conveying a sense of professionalism and care to the church?
- Are we communicating regularly with the congregation and the leaders?
- Is confidentiality on all levels of the project a top concern? Is the analysis team professional in regard to confidentiality? Have we made arrangements to store the surveys in a private place after the project is completed?
- Have we designed the analysis to allow for open-ended input?
- What will we do with information that is not related to the condition of families?
- Have we made allowances for formally and informally gathered data? How will these be integrated into a final report?

Step 9: Analyzing the Data

Once the survey has been administered, it is time for the analysis team to go to work and convert the raw data into meaningful information useful for planning and problem solving. I will describe a method to convert the raw data into report-ready statistics.

For a hand-generated analysis, the survey is administered in the worship assembly. The family minister scans each survey, reads all comments, and notes the feel of the entire set. The surveys are subdivided by age category and assigned to two or three members of the analysis team. The team members tally age group statistics. Each age group is then tallied to produce a grand tally sheet for the entire congregation.

These steps can be accomplished by a tally team of ten computing data for a congregation of one thousand in one afternoon. I believe there are some real benefits for the family minister or the person who will be writing the report to actually read each survey. The writer gets a feel for the needs of the church in a more personal way.

It might be helpful to estimate the time commitment to produce the analysis from Step 9 onward. The minister and the committee may spend approximately one hundred hours in analyzing, writing, editing, and producing the final report. Ministries writing their first report could expect to spend more time.

At this point, you need to integrate the information gathered into the final report. It is exciting to watch a picture of the congregation rise out of the data. Add to that the materials from one-on-one interviews and general observations, and you will struggle to keep the report brief. A good analysis should present some clear parallels between the surveys and the information gathered from other sources.

It is natural to want to hurry through the analysis to the writing of the final report. However, some time should be allocated to let the results soak in. I often spend a few days letting the impact of the survey and interviews rest in my mind. I find that the larger themes will begin to emerge from the data. These themes will serve as the basis for my planning later on.

Step 10: Producing the Final Products

The final report to the congregation and leaders should be written and presented in a clear and concise manner. The report should include the following items:

- Description of the process used—useful when duplicating the process in the future
- The analysis team—who was involved in the analysis and writing of the report
- Major demographics of the church
- The major need areas
- The major training areas
- Long-range goals (twenty-four to thirty-six months)
- Short-range goals (the next twelve months)
- A plan to implement in response to the needs
- How to integrate other ministries to family needs
- Delivery times and methodology
- General recommendations to the entire church

How Do You Present the Report?

Once the status report and the ministry plan of action are completed, the analysis team is ready to present its findings to the church. This is an exciting step as the ministry begins to put flesh and bones on dreams and ideas. Experience has shown that the results should be presented in a variety of formats to communicate the plan to the church.

By this point, you and the analysis team have been immersed in the data for many weeks. You are familiar with the trends and can recite the statistics without looking at them. However, when the report is presented, the lead speaker must address each group from square one.

The presentations should be characterized by clear, simple, and concise speech. The presentations should move briskly through the data but not so fast as to lose the audience. Avoid terminology that is overly statistical. Offer summary statements such as, "The typical young family in this church is like . . . ," or "The major family training is needed in the area of parenting and building faith in the family."

Walk groups through the material in presentation form and with visuals, then hand them the report as they leave. Reports that are given out ahead of time are not read. Reports that are given in the meeting are flipped through, taking the focus off the actual report. Explain to each group exactly how to use the report. Do not assume people will know how to apply the data to their ministry areas.

Speaking with the Leaders

You and the analysis team should plan to meet with the leaders of the church prior to meeting with any other group. A special meeting should be planned that allows for total focus on family ministry.

A multimedia production is the most efficient tool in communicating the status report and the ministry plan in a short period of time. I have frequently used professionally produced slides of all the major findings and the ministry plan of action, and I have found them to be invaluable in communicating to the leadership, staff, and congregation. I strongly recommend the investment of money in a multimedia presentation. A good program can be produced with or without professional narration.

Ask the leaders to set aside several hours to meet with the analysis team. The meeting should cover the major findings of the entire congregation, a breakdown of needs by age group or family type, the ministry plan of action, and a period for questions and answers. This is a great deal of new material to cover in one session, so the ministry might schedule a follow-up meeting for questions or a retreat where more time can be spent digesting the report and its implications.

Whatever the setting, you should ask for feedback from each leader. You may want to construct a feedback form. Each leader should be polled to determine understanding of the data and the plan of action. The level of receptivity must be gauged at that time. This is the point where the ministry moves from foundation setting to raising the walls, and everyone must be ready to work together.

One of the most rewarding experiences is working with the leaders as you move through this process. As they begin to see graphically what their hearts have told them was wrong, the first sense of movement to a solution is felt. The leaders I now work with gave the plan of action a standing ovation around the conference table. They were delighted that we were finally going to do something about the problems of families in the church.

Speaking with the Staff

The second group of people to see the report should be the ministerial staff. In fact, I often leak portions of the report to the staff ahead of time to read in order to brief them on the direction the ministry is going to take.

The entire staff, both full- and part-time members, should be briefed. The format should follow that used with the leaders of the church. The data should be reviewed along with the ministry plan of action using a media presentation. They should receive a copy of the report after the meeting.

The analysis team should prepare some general implications of the report for each major area of ministry. Rather than hand the recommendations to the staff, it is usually preferable to ask each minister to read the report and jot down three or four implications of the report for the area of work. You should then follow up the meeting in about a week with a private conference. Each minister can then share the ideas with you, and you can share the analysis team's recommendations privately with each minister.

Most often, the ministerial staff will welcome the input and be interested in the results. Many may be challenged to use the techniques of needs analysis to more effectively analyze the needs of their own groups. You may serve as a consultant to other ministries as they try to upgrade their ministry plans of action.

Communicating with the Congregation

A successful presentation to the congregation should include prior announcements of the report, the selection of one presenter for the entire report, and a review of the essential data to be presented to the congregation. A one-page summary sheet should be prepared to give persons in attendance that day. Several reports should be available so that members may check them out. The multimedia presentation should be used. One leader of the church should be asked to respond to the report at the end, stating the leadership's approval and endorsement of the plan. The worship service should be planned around the family theme. The entire service should be devoted to the report, and no other program or event should be highlighted that Sunday morning.

Note that I recommend a Sunday morning report. I believe this is the only reasonable time to present the findings. Many will ask if this is appropriate during the worship service. Having done these reports at all hours, I am convinced that a meaningful Sunday morning worship service can be conducted on the day that centers on the design of God's family.

The real motivation for delivering the results on Sunday morning is gaining a consensus of understanding among all family types. The church needs to know its condition. The singles need to hear they are a part of this church. The leaders need a forum to communicate they are truly concerned about being shepherds of God's people. An effective presentation can begin to accomplish these tasks.

Reporting to Bible Class Teachers and Ministry Leaders

In addition to the congregational report and the full status report, I produce a one- or two-page cohort report. This short form will report on the condition of families and families' needs in the twenties, thirties, forties, and so on. This information can be invaluable to Bible class teachers and ministry leaders. No longer do the teachers have to wonder about the most-pressing needs among young couples. They have reliable data.

Teachers and leaders may request a copy of the full report after they have received the one-page summary. The director of adult education may wish to prepare a list of goals and educational objectives for each age grouping or family type based upon the results of the needs analysis.

Our practice has been to recommend the development of a needs-based curriculum for each class. We have followed up the family survey with an educational needs survey in each adult class. With this data in hand, a Bible class teacher has information on how the couples, singles, and families are struggling and where they are in their individual faith development. A set of educational objectives can be created to meet the faith and family needs of each adult Bible class. As you work in conjunction with the adult Bible class director and the staff, you can generate these objectives.

Using Multiple Channels

The family life ministry should capitalize on as many channels of communication as possible to get the message across. People are out of town. A mother is at home with her baby who is ill. A businessman had to work late. There are many reasons why the message may not be heard, but here are a few techniques for sharing the plan with the entire church:

- Write a series of short bulletin articles on the results.
- Write a personal letter to each member.
- Set up a reading room with the report available.
- Hold small group meetings to deliver the plan.
- Rotate through the small groups or Bible classes.

- Meet with the secretaries and support staff.
- Produce a ministry newsletter.
- Ask the minister to preach a series of lessons based on the results.
- Produce a cassette of the report, and make it available.
- Videotape the congregational presentation.

The family life ministry should continually recommunicate its vision to the congregation and the leaders. This will be an ongoing need for the first two to three years.

Inherent Dangers in the Process

Once these steps have been taken, the ministry can be fairly certain of having poured a solid foundation. Several dangers are an inherent part of the needs analysis process, however. By avoiding or addressing these pitfalls, the family ministry will be more successful during its initial year.

Going Too Fast

The most common mistake of ministers is quickly running off three hundred surveys and passing them out at the next available time. Based on this limited data, many premature decisions are made that often must be reversed or waste valuable resources. A needs analysis process is easily a three- to six-month commitment, depending on the size of the congregation and the age of the family life ministry. Pushing deadlines runs the risk of missing important information that takes time to surface.

Making Unwise Choices for the Analysis Team

The job of the project leader is enormous. The person must be able to conceptualize globally and analyze on a detailed level. The person ideally should be an effective presenter, capable of informing the congregation of the plan of action. Finally, the person must have a feel for the internal rules and structures of the church.

The analysis team should reflect a broad range of talents. Gifted men and women with the ability to plan, write, think conceptually, analyze data, and deal with statistics will make key contributions. A good project team should be broad based.

Ignoring Vital Sources of Information

Ministers can use needs analysis to prove their preconceived notions. Periodically, the analysis team should stand back and look at the process to determine if they are gaining information from a wide range of people in the church: Are we ignoring any group or source of information? Is there an area of investigation that has escaped us in the process?

One church hired a Christian counselor to evaluate family needs and make recommendations for ministry and programming. The counselor recommended that the church purchase his seminars and books for the entire program, even though many of his offerings had little to do with the actual needs of the church. It makes little sense to acquire information through a needs analysis process and then ignore it completely.

Gathering Data without Going into the Planning Phase

Surfacing an enormous amount of data without moving into the planning phase is a common error. A solid plan of action with a timetable for its implementation must flow from the data. Remember, needs analysis does not seek information for the sake of curiosity; you are trying to move toward a ministry plan that will meet the needs.

Having One Person Handle the Process

By now it would be clear that the amount of work to effectively complete a needs analysis dictates a team approach. The team provides the time and workpower to complete the project. The team offers a broad-based approach to the analysis. The team prevents errors in interpretation and unnecessary biasing. Finally, a good team builds momentum for launching the plan of action.

Raising Expectations without Delivering the Program

Once a needs analysis is launched, it will raise the level of expectations of the congregation. When members complete a survey, they expect two things. First, they expect to hear from the family minister shortly concerning the results. Second, they expect some, not all, of these needs to be met.

The family minister who hopes to use a needs analysis to motivate reluctant leaders into establishing a family life ministry is playing a deadly game. If the analysis is completed or even begun, the congregation expects some ministry response. A response that never comes sends a negative message to the members. Trying to use a needs analysis to motivate a nonshepherding-oriented leadership into a more pastoral role is doomed to failure. The leadership will entrench, defend its position, and ultimately reject the new ministry.

Failing to Prioritize Needs

Not every need mentioned by the congregation can be met. It is impossible even for the most resourceful church. The analysis team will be forced to make choices and prioritize some needs. This means finding alternative methods of dealing with some problems and putting some well-intentioned ideas on the back burner.

One of the most frustrating problems for the family minister is the sheer lack of time to implement all the suggested programs. Focusing resources on some main objectives is necessary. I often advise churches that do not have a full-time person working in this area to focus on one or two objectives each year and feel good about the efforts they are making.

Pointing to the Church's Needs That the Leader Would Rather Not Know

This relates to the opening story of our chapter. Some staffs and leaders do not want to know the condition of their families. The truth may alter their concepts too drastically. It may force the admission that congregational priorities are out of focus. It may surface personal issues and family struggles in their lives that have remained buried and carefully protected.

Whatever the reason, you must move cautiously if you perceive that leaders are moving away from or moving against the process. Read this movement carefully before blindly opposing it. Some churches are more content ignoring real problems. Others would rather bemoan the fact that we have not re-created the good old days than seriously pursue an active ministry to families.

Bringing Conflict to the Surface

Sometimes the family needs analysis surfaces congregational conflict that has remained buried for many years. The members have not been given a voice, and the survey is the first feedback tool they have had in years. When comments are asked for, comments are given! The flow of emotions can be overwhelming.

In this instance you are called upon to hear the needs of the entire congregational system. Usually, however, you do not have the positional power or responsibility to effect any necessary change.

This is a highly tenuous position to be in. The church may have been expending a great deal of effort to keep the conflict buried or hidden.

You have several options. First, you may ignore the nonfamilial comments as not being a part of the study or your responsibility. Second, you may take the information and try to respond personally, circumventing the leaders. Third, you may act as an honest broker and inform the leaders of these trends and suggest some useful paths to take.

Experience has shown that when conflict arises through the needs analysis and it is significant enough to warrant attention, the third option provides a reasonable path for the minister and the analysis team. The name of a church consultant could be recommended as a part of the final recommendations of the committee. Trying to respond to these needs without the support of the leaders of the church places the minister in a role that is open to criticism from all sides. Church conflict can be resolved only when all sides are willing to sit down and discuss differences and options.

A Final Word

We have covered a great deal of material related to effective needs analysis. The time spent in this phase is worth the effort. We have observed that the needs analysis requires support and involvement from all levels of the leadership. The family life minister must gather the internal expertise to see the project to completion. Once completed, the analysis will certainly help direct the ministry and raise the likelihood of more effectively meeting the needs of the people. Needs analysis becomes another tool in the ministerial tool kit. The church doesn't need another shelved report that was interesting but effected little change.

6

MODELS OF FAMILY LIFE MINISTRY

I arrived at the church offices just as the sun was coming up over the city. As a second-year graduate student, I had come to town to try to find one church interested in ministering to families. Under my arm, I carried a small notebook with the working papers that represented what I believed to be a workable model for a local church—if only someone would listen.

"We're doing all that you're talking about," said one minister politely. Yet as I walked out, I noticed on the membership board there were very few young couples and children to replenish the ranks.

"The church has no business doing this sort of thing," replied another minister.

But this morning it might be different. Perhaps this young and energetic fellow leading a growing church in the suburbs would listen. He said, "Sounds like a great idea, but it's really not the direction we're going right now. Thanks for the visit."

Ten years later offered a new perspective. The first church I visited closed its early childhood education wing. The congregation had not birthed any young families with children. It was aging gracefully and quietly. The second church lost the minister, who had family problems, a short time after he lectured me. The third church invited me to design a ministry model for them ten years later. One-third of the adult members reported a need for counseling in the family. The ten-year delay had taken a heavy toll.

I have defined family life ministry and presented the various decisions that church leaders must make to initiate a new ministry. I have described the programming process that identifies the needs of the church. Now I want to focus on the development of the ministry model. All the groundwork and research should be done. It is time to bring on-line a family ministry that is targeted and relevant.

Many leaders scratch their heads at this point and ask, "What do we do first?" The needs identified in the analysis may seem overwhelming. No one may have a vision for what the end product is supposed to look like, yet everyone agrees on the need to do something!

This chapter offers a developmental model of family life ministry. We will look at a basic structure that incorporates inreach, a ministry to the local church, and outreach. We will consider steps that any church can take to minister to its families, especially churches that do not have a full-time family minister or a budget. We will examine a model of family life ministry that integrates itself with existing ministries of the church. We will explore a fully developed program targeted toward the community. Finally, we will see a network model designed to move the local church into the role of a community resource provider.

None of these models is exhaustive. They are, just as the name implies, models of what can be done. I offer them as a beginning point for fruitful thought for the family life minister and the leadership. Family ministry programs will not, and should not, be identical in all churches. Emphasis and opportunities will define the ministry in each church. Some ministries will be focused toward inreach. Others will target the community. Staff and resource considerations will create openings and constraints.

The critical point is, each church can do something! From the largest to the smallest, every congregation of God's people can do something to minister to families.

I was thrilled with the initiative shown by a lawyer who attended one of my family ministry seminars. He took extensive notes on needs analysis and programming. He asked questions and went home committed to implementing family life ministry in his home congregation. About a year later, I received a ministry plan of action authored by the man and his new family ministry committee. He went home, did his reading and homework, and initiated his own family needs analysis. He and a few committed members convinced the leaders of their ideas and their ability to do it themselves!

It is possible to build an excellent family life ministry with limited resources. The greatest resources God has given us are our commitment to Him and our creativity. As you read this chapter, let your creative juices flow. Imagine your model for your church. Do not duplicate—create!

A General Model of Ministry

When I first began ministering to families, I needed a conceptual framework to help me visualize what I was trying to do and how I was going to do it. I began by seeing myself and my ministry team as initiating leaders. No one really knew what we were trying to build, so I knew we had to function as initiating leaders. I also knew that my first job was to identify the needs of the local church and translate the needs into goals and objectives. We have already discussed this process in great detail (see fig. 6.1).

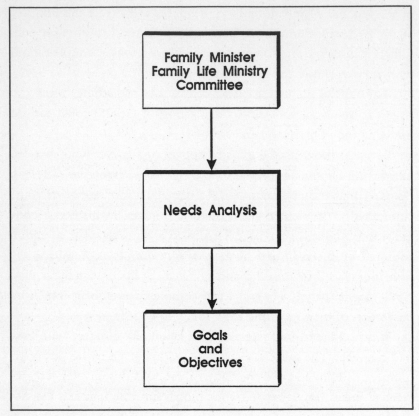

Fig. 6.1. A general model of ministry

It was a dynamic model. In other words, each element had an impact on every other element. We were influencing the needs analysis through our observations, and the needs analysis was influencing us. We knew we had to make a decision. We had to decide whether we were going to target inreach or outreach first. Our resources would not permit both. After discussions with our leaders, we decided to target outreach first. Our model contained two new elements (see fig. 6.2).

We discussed various ministry opportunities. We decided that counseling was a major need, and it would be one of the first requests made by people attending any class or seminar. This proved to be a wise decision.

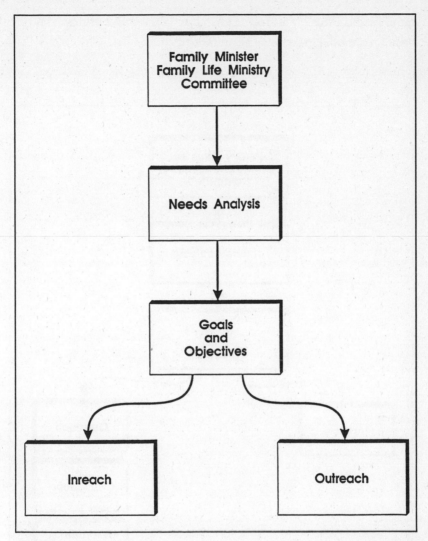

Fig. 6.2.

We also decided to dedicate a regular weekly class to family life issues and design it to be guest friendly. Our hope was that church members would see the relevance of our topics and invite their friends and coworkers. We then decided to author one or two special seminars designed to meet the needs of dual-career and single-parent families and offer them free of charge to interested businesses in our area. Our model grew once again (see fig. 6.3).

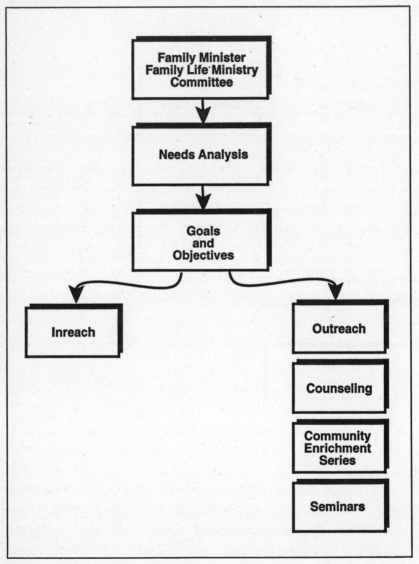

Fig. 6.3.

At this point we felt the need to create the backbone of any family life ministry, the resource center. We needed good materials to build our ministry around. We added special events, an occasional community focused worship service or series, and a special group of businessmen and businesswomen who helped us make contacts in the professional community. By the time we realized what had happened, our model had grown to a very broad-based outreach program intent on reaching the urban family we considered to be unchurched but Christian friendly (see fig. 6.4).

Our family ministry had grown like a junior high school boy over the summer holidays. But all was not well on the home front. Some of our members were feeling neglected: "Here we are helping all of these other folks, and we are not even taking care of our own church family. Doesn't the Bible say to do good to all people, especially those of the household of faith?" I had been reprimanded and stood guilty as charged. I learned my first lesson in model building. Take time out for the home church first.

We learned the hard way that our church family wanted some of the dessert, too! They felt neglected and ignored. We designed the counseling, classes, and seminars to be open to anyone who wanted to attend, but we had not consciously pastored our people. We had not taken the time to help them feel the special gifts of the ministry. We quickly regrouped and designed a complement of programs to meet the needs of our members. We returned to our needs analysis and started targeting inreach goals.

We were concerned that an emphasis on inreach would hamper our outreach efforts. Would we become self-serving navel gazers? The answer was comforting and surprising. Many of the structures we had created could be retooled and turned toward the local church for inreach purposes. We did not have to create many new ministries; we just had to retarget the existing ones. In some cases, we needed only internal communications to make everyone aware of what was available. We added a component on faith development

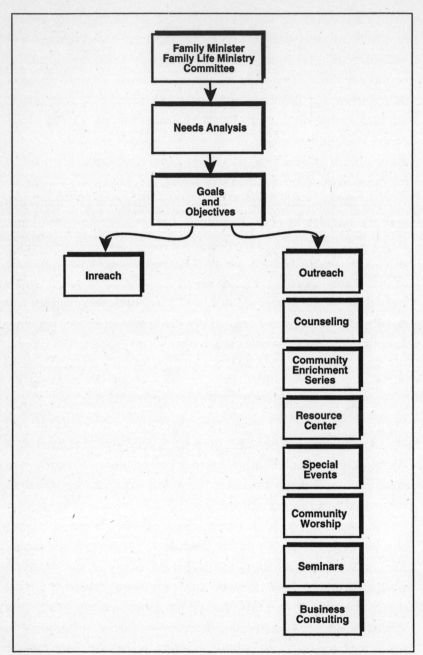

Fig. 6.4.

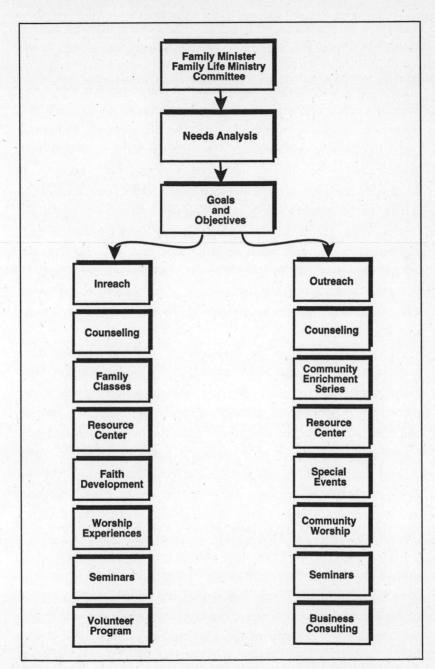

Fig. 6.5.

that was a special concern for our members and initiated a general model of ministry that accomplished both inreach and outreach (see fig. 6.5).

After we developed a more comprehensive inreach model for our church, we began to see a dynamic interrelationship between the two parts of the program. In other words, as we expanded our outreach to the community, our opportunities for inreach and integration of new members into the church increased. Furthermore, as we concentrated on inreach, our members became convinced of the validity of the ministry and began doing more effective outreach. We created, quite accidentally, a family ministry model where inreach and outreach accomplished their individual goals and also fed each other. The relationship between inreach and outreach deepened and attention to one area normally led to residual benefits in the other. The interrelationship can be represented by the arrows between the two goals (see fig. 6.6).

The final chapter in the development of this model occurred several years after its start. As we evaluated our progress and our programs, we discovered new insights into the goals and purposes of our ministry. The information was vital in redefining our efforts. Inreach and outreach had a dynamic influence on the overall goals and purposes of the ministry. In other words, the practice of the ministry defined the goals of the ministry. We learned to stop periodically and evaluate what we were doing and its impact on the church or community. Our model added a feedback loop into the goals and objectives of our ministry (see fig. 6.7).

This model of family ministry can be generalized to many situations. The individual elements under inreach and outreach can be interchanged with other offerings, depending on the unique situation of the church. The fact remains, if a ministry targets the church and the community, a dynamic relationship can be developed that will be beneficial to both. Let's consider what can be done by a church without a full- or part-time family life minister to assist families.

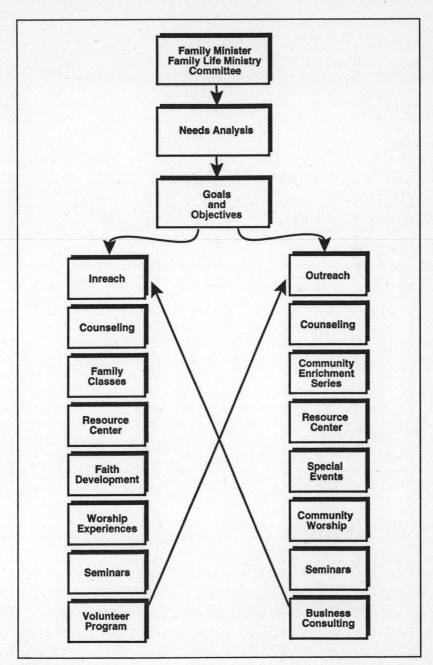

Fig. 6.6.

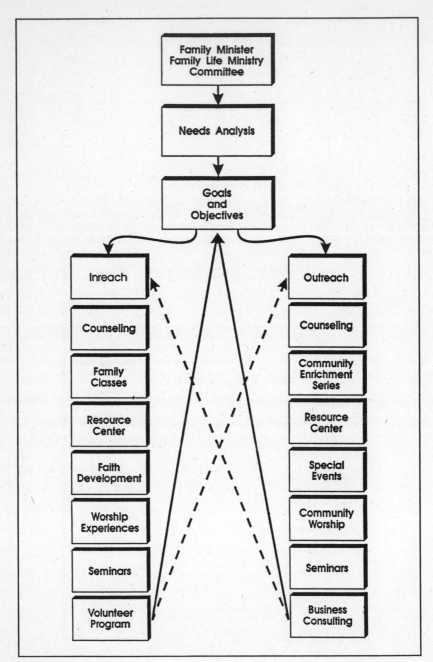

Fig. 6.7.

Initiating the Ministry without a
Family Life Minister

A congregation does not need a full- or part-time family life minister to do family life ministry. What is needed is a commitment by leaders and members to help families prepare for and deal with crises.

In the remainder of this chapter, we will be discussing a developmental model for family life ministry. The model can begin without any staff help and grow to the point where a staff minister needs to provide leadership. If the ministry continues to grow, a full-time minister may be hired to devote full energies to this work.

I propose an eight-stage model of development. These stages represent the major developmental phases that a growing family life ministry can go through. Not every family ministry will be capable of fulfilling all the tasks of each stage (a part-time committee cannot do as much as a full-time minister), but it will offer a framework to build the ministry around. The stages are sequential. That is, it is important to complete one stage before moving on to the next.

Each stage addresses a major question. The answer or answers to this question will produce a ministry product. That is, there will be something tangible to show for energies expended in each stage.

Stage 1:	Referral	What help can be immediately rallied?
Stage 2:	Resources	What resources can be quickly applied?
Stage 3:	Retooling	What continuing education do we need?
Stage 4:	Research	What is the condition of our families?
Stage 5:	Remediation	What counseling do we offer?
Stage 6:	Reeducation	What education/enrichment do we offer?
Stage 7:	Reconstruction	What impact will the ministry have on the larger church family system?
Stage 8:	Reaching Out	How shall we reach out?

Let's consider each stage separately before applying all of them to the church that does not have a full-time family minister.

Stage 1: Referral
What Help Can Be Immediately Rallied?

It is a good idea to begin by addressing the need for counseling up front. I call this building the backstop. Every church should have a backstop of good counseling resources to refer members to. It will lay the groundwork for an effective referral network so important in Stage 5.

My first Monday morning in Atlanta is forever etched in my mind. I was scheduled to attend a staff meeting at nine o'clock. Shortly after I showered, the phone rang. It was a call for counseling. We chatted for a while and set up an appointment. Almost immediately the phone rang again, another urgent call for counseling from a member. Before reaching the staff meeting, I had received six calls for professional help. I was late for the meeting, and I realized I was going to be late in setting up help that could be quickly rallied for the people.

Some churches will struggle with the backstop issue. Counselors may not be readily available. Community resources may not be known. I find many churches are isolated from the help around them in their own community. It is well worth the time and effort to investigate the counselors in your area.

Geographically isolated or small congregations may wish to consider joining with other congregations to bring in a counselor to work with them on alternate days. Three or four churches could easily share one rotating counselor and all benefit from the plan. Family ministry offers an excellent opportunity to build congregational interaction. Many universities are training professionals who are committed to working in local church settings. Some of these programs are open to placing an intern in a local church setting.

The intern would provide low-cost counsel under graduate supervision, and the church would receive high-quality but affordable services.

Stage 2: Resources
What Resources Can Be Quickly Applied?

This question illustrates the need for the family ministry to be ready to provide resources at the very outset. The resources may be as basic as a reading shelf in the church library or a list of community agencies that offer counseling. The point is, the mere announcement of the formation of a family ministry committee will often initiate requests for help from the congregation. The process of acquiring and disseminating information about local resources is an ongoing task of the family life ministry.

Stage 3: Retooling
What Continuing Education Do We Need?

The explosion of family problems has heightened the need for extensive and ongoing training for anyone working with local congregations in a pastoring role. The family life ministry should be a pace setter in ongoing, challenging continuing education. Training should focus on family ministry in general along with people helping, counseling for church leaders, addictions, marriage, and current topics in family relations. Special attention should be given to helping the leader develop a better understanding of the family of origin and the issues that may be present in personal life.

The congregation should also be provided with top quality continuing education. Many colleges and universities offer short courses and noncredit training tracks for lay leaders. But the whole church can become a more caring Christian community through training in listening skills, encouragement, and healthy faith development. Fortune 500 companies provide training and development for their people. We should do no less for the kingdom of God. Our people are our most valuable family enrichment resource.

Stage 4: Research
What Is the Condition of Our Families?

Most churches will begin with a congregational needs analysis, but some may want to include a neighborhood survey as well. The end product of this stage would be a status report on the condition of families in the church or community along with a ministry plan of action.

Stage 5: Remediation
What Counseling Do We Offer?

In Stage 1, I suggested building a backstop to buy time for the ministry to ascertain where it is going. This is the point to move from building a backstop to constructing a stadium. You will have detailed information on the needs of families "headed for the waterfalls" and will have some idea of the possible counseling options the church can generate. In Stage 5, you want to decide upon and implement a long-term counseling strategy that will meet current and future needs.

Stage 6: Reeducation
What Education/Enrichment Do We Offer?

By this stage, the ministry is taking shape with classes, seminars, retreats, and other events being planned as a part of the regular programming. Many churches will choose to specialize in either counseling or prevention at this point. Others will choose to continue to offer both.

Stage 7: Reconstruction
What Impact Will the Ministry Have on the Larger Church Family System?

By the time the ministry enters this stage, it is mature. The programs and counseling have built a trust relationship. The congregation has discussed the implications of becoming a faith family. You, the family minister, are ready to act as a more aggressive champion for family ministry in the area of systemic family rules within the larger church structure.

You and the family ministry committee may call for changes in programming, goals, and even values within the church family. You may point out traditions that are maladaptive to building healthy families. You may suggest new festivals and celebrations to be marker events in a markerless age. Whatever the changes, large or small, every church needs a champion to guard and protect the needs of the individual family. The ability to address needed systemic changes is based on the integrity and competence of the family life minister and the track record of the ministry itself. Attempting to alter systemic family rules early on is often counterproductive.

Stage 8: Reaching Out
How Shall We Reach Out?

You are now concerned with reaching out to your neighbors and friends as a primary thrust of the ministry. The groundwork has been laid to upgrade the staff, leadership, and congregational skills in the area of family relations. You have built a backstop of counseling resources and prepared preventive offerings. You have taken the time to look at yourselves and your community and targeted some needs that you feel comfortable and qualified to address in the local church.

It takes time to develop the skills and leadership necessary to move through all eight stages. In fact, I believe it would be unwise for a church without a full-time minister to families to attempt it.

Returning to the original question concerning a church without a full- or part-time family life minister, I suggest it apply the model by attempting to fulfill the tasks outlined in Stages 1, 2, and 3 only (see fig. 6.8).

Stage	No Staff
Referral	Yes
Resources	Yes
Retooling	Yes
Research	Possible
Remediation	Option
Reeducation	Option
Reconstruction	_____
Reaching out	_____

Fig. 6.8. Family life ministry
Eight-stage developmental model—no staff

A church could build an effective family life ministry by concentrating on referrals, resources, and retooling the leaders and the congregation. These three goals would provide some level of competent care within the church without a large expenditure of money for budgets or salaries. It would also lay the groundwork for the church to build into a second level of growth where a staff minister might assume the duties of a family life minister along with another role.

After accomplishing most of the tasks in Stages 1, 2, and 3, the family ministry would be ready to conduct research on the local church or community. The direction of this research would need to be dictated by the decision to emphasize remediation or reeducation. I do not believe it is wise for a young, lay-led family life ministry to attempt to build a family ministry that offers both prevention and therapy. One or the other should be chosen. Most committee-led ministries will do a great deal of good and grow significantly by opting for either prevention or therapy.

One church decided to begin a family ministry through the efforts of some highly committed members. They defined a preventive direction for their ministry because several counselors and a counseling center were readily available to church members. With limited resources they produced and distributed a high-quality family newsletter. Various members of the church wrote articles. Relevant books were reviewed, and information was given on marriage, parenting, and many other topics. Church members began sharing the newsletter with friends, and requests came from people in the community to be added to the mailing list each month. With a targeted emphasis on prevention and a high-quality execution of one method—a newsletter—the church was able to do something positive in family ministry.

In summary, the direction for a lay-led family life ministry would include the following goals: (1) develop and educate the family ministry team; (2) build an effective referral base for counseling; (3) access available preventive resources; and (4) initiate discussions of a preventive or therapeutic emphasis as the ministry grows.

What Any Church Can Do to Minister to Its Families

Church leaders often ask me to describe highly successful and low-cost programming ideas that can be incorporated into the local church. Here are some ideas to begin a low-cost family life ministry.

Create a standing committee on family life and ministry.

Ask the committee to review the life of the church, programming, emphasis, pastoral care, and care of the leaders. Charge them with the responsibility of guarding the sanctity of the home and not allowing the demands of the local church to grow beyond manageability. This group would become the nucleus of the family life ministry and the leadership team for a full-time minister.

Make a habit of reading family-oriented literature and buying materials for the leaders.

Family ministry is built upon reading and listening skills. There are many instructive books on how the church and the family can join hands and promote health for both groups. These should be read and discussed. I often purchase reading copies for my fellow staff members and other church leaders. Occasionally, it is a good idea to prepare summary papers of major books or concepts to provide leaders who may not have the opportunity to read as widely as the family life committee.

Acquire books and tapes for a resource shelf.

In some churches, the loneliest place in the building is the church library. It contains the rejects from past ministers' libraries and donations from well-meaning members. It is the harbinger of out-of-date materials. Why not excite your church library with the regular purchase of new books on some family theme? Make it a small line item in the budget. Print the titles in the bulletin each month. Each time the congregation gets together, have a resource advisor in the library to consult with members.

Set up a resource and referral table in the foyer.

I believe the best program a beginning family life ministry can offer to its members without any up-front cost is a resource and referral table in the foyer. Stock it with books available to be purchased, tape series, family magazines, and Christian children's books and videos. Provide a listing of counselors and support groups in your area that are available to help families in crises. Staff it with family life committee members who are available to answer questions and make recommendations.

Start a regular family life class as a part of the Bible school offerings each week.

Train your church that classes addressing the needs of families are an integral part of a holistic Bible school program. You need not have highly trained experts. Many family life courses are written with excellent leaders' guides. Consider a current best-seller, and buy everyone in the class a copy. Spend the quarter discussing a chapter each night. Many are written in a thirteen-week format. Consider the use of videotapes. For a fairly reasonable fee, your church can purchase a video of some of the best experts in the field of family studies. Use them as discussion starters. Some churches are buying satellite hookups that will allow them the option of accessing national speakers in their classrooms. Two-way phone conversations are allowing student-teacher interaction. Many larger churches are producing instructional videos that can be borrowed, rented, or purchased. Consider the options in your area. With the technological advances of the past decades, there really is no such thing as an isolated church; there is only isolated thinking.

Offer a yearly family life series on a topic of critical concern to the church.

A yearly family life series can help the church address some of the more pressing family concerns of members. Any church can set aside one month to emphasize the family in its programming. Members can invite friends and use the weekend as an outreach tool. The theme for the weekend can be generated by a needs analysis conducted in the Sunday morning Bible classes. A quality resource speaker can deliver theme lectures or classes.

The family life series concept can be expanded to a full family life conference for the church. Several speakers and multiple learning tracks can be offered. For instance, a church might offer a main track on building self-esteem in the family while offering specialized studies in parenting, parenting young children, parenting teens, coping with the empty nest, and so on. Participants would attend the main lecture and then choose the special interest class that matches their family situation.

Some churches are reclaiming the Christian calendar for the family. They build their family life ministry around the natural events of the calendar year. Fall becomes a time of enrichment as children and college students go back to school. Christmas is a time of reflection and the renewal of family ties. Summer becomes a time of celebration and reunion. Though I have never organized my family life ministry in this way, I believe it has a great deal to offer because it follows the natural rhythm of the family throughout the year. Programming follows the natural interests of the family.

Invest in training for core family ministry leaders.

Training for core family ministry leaders is essential to build a healthy initiating team. Many times lay leaders feel they have to be trained psychologists to be a part of the ministry. Nothing could be further from the truth. With training, many church members can make significant contributions to the family ministry.

Many colleges and universities have recognized the need to provide ongoing training for returning adult students with short courses, audit courses, and off-site educational opportunities. Many graduate school professors will come to the local church and teach a condensed version of one of their courses. We took our entire leadership team through a weekend seminar, "Counseling for Church Leaders." The training was especially geared for the leader who wants some basic counseling knowledge without having a degree or becoming a full-time therapist. An instructor from a university thousands of miles away was selected based upon his expertise. The training was handled in-house and scheduled around our people's calendars. Many ways exist to challenge church members educationally, and I have found that most members welcome the opportunity to improve their understanding.

Submit and justify a yearly budget.

Most churches can allocate funds for family life programming. Make this a regular line item in the budget, and justify your programming expenses at the end of the year. Show church leaders the effectiveness of spending money on preventive family programming. Ask members to submit written evaluations of the programs they attend. Ask for feedback from class attendees, and share it with your leaders. Plan for growth, and submit more aggressive budgets once the need has been established. If leaders can catch a vision for what can be accomplished through a family life ministry, the ministry will grow.

Some churches have chosen to fund family life ministry as a part of the local outreach and evangelism efforts. Local missions are seen as quality family life classes being offered to the community through direct mail, advertising in the local paper, or friend-to-friend contact.

Contact local real estate agents and marketing groups for demographics of your area that can be purchased at a minimal cost.

I am amazed at the amount of information available on communities if we access it through the appropriate people. When I prepared to move to Atlanta, I announced to one of my graduate classes in counseling that I was leaving the area. One student, a marketing major retraining to be a psychotherapist, said she had been working for a restaurant chain that was opening twelve new stores in the northern Atlanta region. She offered to check with her superiors and get permission to share their entire market analysis with us free of charge. We gained priceless information from a corporate source that was happy to help out once the management learned we were trying to help families.

Real estate agents, local chambers of commerce, local newspapers, and advertising/marketing groups can provide vital data to any church wanting to research the community. Some churches will want to invest in community profile reports. These services provide a profile of the target area from a one-, five-, and ten-mile perspective. They offer demographics on the families living in the community. Some offer descriptions of the various households that do not require a degree in statistics to understand. For the money, I have found these reports to be well worth the investment compared to the research I can generally produce.

Travel to other churches and view their programs.

A church can begin a family life ministry by sending a representative to existing family life ministries to spend a day on an on-site interview. Seeing how someone else has invented the wheel is beneficial.

Visits could include churches that are comparable in size and complexity to the home congregation. However, you might gain vital programming insights by visiting churches that are larger or smaller. An inner-city church that ministers to its families might have some excellent insights that a suburban church needs to know. Care should be taken, however, not to take the ministry conducted at one church and transplant it in another location. View the church and the ministry as unique. Try to uncover the principles that make a particular ministry work in a particular location. You may be able to transfer these principles.

Expand the impact of family problems by including church leaders in the remedial process.

Sometimes church leaders feel the strain of family problems from a general standpoint, but they do not feel it on a daily basis. I have found that asking a church leader to walk with me through a case, a family crisis, or a referral heightens the appreciation of the need for family life ministry.

Get on mailing lists of conferences and lectures.

The family ministry committee may decide to attend a national or regional family conference each year. Other ministries with limited resources may not be able to travel, or work schedules may exclude key leaders in the ministry. The family minister can provide excellent continuing education materials through purchasing conference tapes and videos and making them available to leaders. Many universities, graduate schools, and publishers produce taped resources that can enrich the ministry.

Purchase prepared family enrichment materials featuring train-the-trainer guides.

Many curricula provide marriage and family enrichment materials for the nonprofessional teacher. Family life ministries can train trainers and group facilitators using materials prepared by leading experts in the field. It is not necessary to have a formal degree to provide these classes.

Courses are packaged in a variety of formats including videotape and audiotape. Many include participant guides, and the best-designed courses also supply a leader's packet. These leaders' guides are priceless for the growing ministry. They will help the lay leader structure a class for a thirteen-week quarter system, a weekend retreat, or a seminar. Most come with resources for further study and preparation. The more complete packages offer contact people to assist with questions or the implementation of the program. Any church can take the issues surfaced in the needs analysis and provide a basic preventive course to address those concerns.

A lay-led family life ministry would emphasize referrals, resources, and retooling. It would be possible to conduct some basic research on the internal needs of the congregation. The ministry would likely need to opt for an emphasis on remediation or reeducation due to limited full-time resources. However, I have suggested over a dozen options for the church to pursue from a programming standpoint that will cost very little financially but will address the felt needs of the people.

Now that a basis for family ministry has been laid, a staff minister will likely need to devote some time on a daily basis to the ministry. The next stage explores how to continue the development of the ministry when the minister wears two hats. We will explore how to integrate the ministry and protect the minister from becoming overloaded.

Developing Family Life Ministry with a Combination Minister

A combination minister refers to any staff position that combines the work of family ministry with another ministry specialization. Typical combinations are youth and family or education and family. Many pulpit ministers are working toward combining their effort with a family emphasis, and I believe this is an excellent idea.

Returning to our eight-stage model, we find the ministry ready to expand to three additional major areas of work: research, remediation, and reeducation. Although these areas may have had some attention in a lay-led ministry, they should develop fully under staff direction. There is usually no reason why the ministry cannot offer both prevention and therapy at this point (see fig. 6.9).

The family ministry with a part-time family life minister can expand its goals and services. Likely, the ministry will still focus primarily on the local church with some outreach being accomplished through the individual members. It will be possible for the minister to lead the family ministry through a comprehensive family needs analysis if that has not already been done. Both preventive and therapeutic programs should be developed to meet various needs within the church.

There are many pros and cons of having a combination family life minister. Most churches will not be in a financial state to offer a full-time position, so flexibility is important.

Here are some of the major benefits:

• It allows for easier integration of the program into existing ministries.

Stage	No Staff	Combination Minister
Referral	Yes	Yes
Resources	Yes	Yes
Retooling	Yes	Yes
Research	Possible	Yes
Remediation	Option	Yes
Reeducation	Option	Option
Reconstruction	————	————
Reaching out	————	————

Fig. 6.9. Family life ministry
Eight-stage developmental model—combination minister

- The minister is often on staff already and with some retooling could develop an effective ministry in this area.
- A minister who is already on staff may have an understanding of the families to be served and the resources available.
- It provides the minister an enriching way to expand the ministry.

Here are some of the major drawbacks:

- The minister may quickly begin to feel overwhelmed by wearing too many hats.
- The ministry may have difficulty moving beyond the four walls of the church. (This is valid ministry, however!)

• There is a danger in taking the title-only approach and not receiving adequate additional education.

Understanding the impact of the last drawback is important. I know of several churches that have expanded their youth minister's role to a youth and family title. It is nothing more than a title. These well-meaning individuals offer their services as family ministers without adequate background and training.

Ministers who attach the title *family minister* to their names in any form automatically attach certain congregational expectations. Normally, these expectations center on counseling abilities. My ministry friends will protest, "Oh, no, Dr. Don, we minister to the entire family. We are not trained counselors." My experience has been that ministers who carry the title also carry certain expectations. The questions and calls for assistance will come. Family ministers must have training in counseling appropriate to the problems they are being called upon to assist with. If they do not, they should not add the title.

Churches should consider carefully the movement of a staff minister into family life ministry. A combination ministry can be very satisfying to the church and the minister if it is initiated with the proper planning. This suggested sequence of eight major steps would move the church into a combination family life ministry:

Step 1:   Complete the preliminary decisions needed on the leadership level of the church.

Step 2:   Build consensus with the congregation to determine if family ministry is a viable option for the church.

Step 3:   Appoint a family ministry committee, and conduct an appropriate feasibility study.

   a)   Carry out a needs analysis.

   b)   Evaluate current resources in the church and community.

   c)   Conduct a rigorous evaluation of staff giftedness.

Step 4: Develop options based on the feasibility study.

Option 1: We are not able to develop a family ministry due to lack of resources—time, people, finances.

Option 2: We are not able to develop family ministry now but could work with another congregation.

Option 3: We will pursue family ministry with a staff minister to be retooled and reassigned in a combination role.

Option 4: We will pursue family ministry by hiring an additional minister to do family ministry and one other role.

Step 5: Select an option, and implement it for a specified period of time with appropriate review.

Step 6: Redefine job expectations if the minister is adding an additional hat.

a) Enlist the minister's help in the redefinition.

b) Involve members or staff ministers in filling the gaps.

c) Put the changes in writing along with a review date with the personnel committee.

d) Communicate the changes to the congregation.

Step 7: Provide additional resources for the family life ministry as dictated by the minister and committee.

Step 8: Review the needs analysis, and set a reasonable one-year plan based on the following factors: the needs of the church, the resources that can be brought to bear, the time and talents of the minister, and the demands of the additional ministry area.

Once these eight steps have been taken, a review of the situation at six and twelve months is vital. It is all too typical to turn a ministry over to someone and then never follow up until the person burns out or does something wrong. This is poor management. The combination family life minister is one of the most stressful ministerial positions to occupy, and most churches should not plan on keeping a person in that slot for a very long time.

The Challenge of the Full Family Ministry Program

Once a church has devoted itself to the first two phases of development, it will be natural to consider a full-time minister and move to a fully developed family life ministry. The timetable for the growth and development will differ from congregation to congregation, but the assignment of a full-time person to this area will open many doors to community outreach.

Moving to a full program also opens up the final two stages in our developmental model: reconstruction and outreach.

Reconstruction refers to the ministry's ability to help the members and the leaders interpret the rules, decisions, and traditions in light of what is best for the individual families in the church. It assists in initiating new traditions. It functions as a champion for the needs of all families in the church.

Outreach is taking the family ministry into the community for the purpose of service and Christian action. Outreach can be effective only with a healthy church body. An unhealthy church family will screen out members of the community and treat them as "aliens and strangers in the land."

Both stages require the family minister to lead with the trust and cooperation of the leaders of the church. These stages cannot be effectively implemented in the early development of a family life ministry.

We now have a complete eight-stage program developed carefully with the needs of the church and community clearly in mind (see fig. 6.10).

Stage	No Staff	Combination Minister	Full-time Minister
Referral	Yes	Yes	Yes
Resources	Yes	Yes	Yes
Retooling	Yes	Yes	Yes
Research	Possible	Yes	Yes
Remediation	Option	Yes	Yes
Reeducation	Option	Option	Yes
Reconstruction	_____	_____	Yes
Reaching out	_____	_____	Yes

Fig. 6.10. Family life ministry
Eight-stage developmental model—full-time minister

A Program Example

Figure 6.11 illustrates a family life ministry that was developed following the eight-stage sequence. It features a counseling center, a preventive educational program called Prepare, community outreach, a spiritual development ministry called the Family Altar, business consulting, and consulting with churches interested in ministering to families.

Let's examine each of these ministries in more detail. What purpose does it serve? What is the rationale for its existence? What direction and leadership does it require? What are the resource needs of each area?

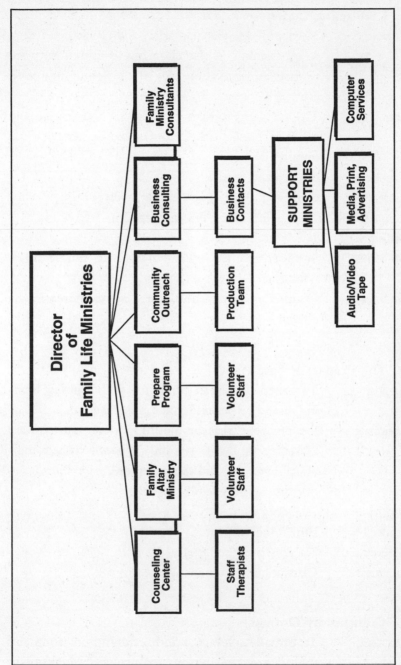

Fig. 6.11. Full program profile

Counseling Center

Purpose: To provide individual, marital, and family counseling to all families in the church and community for restoration of relationships in the family and with God.

Rationale: The congregational needs analysis and community needs survey should document the existence of this ministry.

Direction: Inreach and outreach

Leadership: Clinical director of counseling services

Support staff: Therapeutic staff—full and part time

Additional
ministries: Support groups, referral networks, scholarships, bookstore

Facilities: Counseling center, bookstore, resource area in the church

The Prepare Program

Purpose: To provide Christian family life skills training; training should be preventive and proactive.

Rationale: It is our belief that the most important stance toward Christian family life is a proactive one to help individuals, couples, and families prepare for the stresses of contemporary family living.

Direction: Inreach

Leadership: Family life minister

Support staff: Trainers, other ministers

Facilities: Classrooms and seminar space

Community Outreach

Purpose: To provide relevant, nonthreatening environments for unchurched persons to receive contemporary messages and training on family issues of vital concern to build bridges for Christian service and concern.

Rationale: Our experience has shown that community guests are open to relevant teaching on the struggles of contemporary families from a biblical standpoint. The delivery of programs in a nonthreatening and meaningful way has been shown to open the door for deeper discussion of spiritual concerns.

Direction: Outreach
Leadership: Family life minister
Support staff: Community outreach team
Facilities: On-site or off-site from the church

Family Altar Ministry

Purpose: To provide the church with a strong emphasis in personal and familial faith development through the spiritual disciplines.

Rationale: The needs analysis has documented the "faith in family" theme as a major need of families.

Direction: Inreach primarily
Leadership: Family life minister or women's group minister
Support staff: Family altar team
Facilities: None in addition to the church

Business Consulting

Purpose: To provide businesses with the resources to cope with the changing American family and its impact on the workplace, and to integrate the balance of work, home, and church.

Rationale: No one societal change has had such a dramatic impact on the American family as the change in the nature of work in one generation. The family ministry must help church members and community businesses strengthen the family unit.

Direction: Outreach

Leadership: Family life minister

Support staff: Businesspeople in the church and community

Facilities: None additional needed

Family Ministry Consultants

Purpose: To provide other churches and mission points with the tools to effectively minister to their families through family life ministry.

Rationale: Many churches will be unable to afford even a part-time staff person to address the needs of families. Regional churches can adopt a resource center attitude and make their programs and materials available to other ministers in the area.

Direction: Outreach

Leadership: Family life minister

Support staff: Production team

Facilities: None additional needed

This is just one form that a fully developed family life ministry could take. Each church and each situation will require new and innovative thinking to master the opportunities available. There is one final stage that a family ministry and church can enter in an effort to minister to families in the local church.

The Networking Model

Some churches because of their geographic location or visionary leadership will be in a position to network with many church and parachurch organizations in the community. These churches will move beyond inreach and outreach to become driving forces in the entire community to build strong families. They will be looked to in both religious and secular communities as lighthouses of guidance for building families in the coming years.

These networking churches will define their role as a clearinghouse of church and parachurch services that benefit entire cities. They will cultivate a reputation as churches that really care about families. They will be looked to as leaders in family life education and ministry. Their services will be of the highest quality so as to be sought after by the private sector, including businesses, industries, and city governments.

Networking churches will bring together leaders in many fields of family service to offer a comprehensive package of programs from cradle to grave. Not that they will initiate all of these programs, but they will serve as a conduit between those who are suffering and the services that can meet their needs.

Figure 6.12 illustrates one possible model of a networking church in a large urban area. The areas may change, but the opportunities are almost limitless, including internal ministries, parachurch ministries, and public service organizations.

Large urban areas will come to depend upon megachurches with highly sophisticated family life ministries that are networked with programs and services throughout the city, the region, and the country. No longer are family ministers confined to the ministry of members in their own backyards. We will see an increase in the number of requests for help and consultation from outlying regions and other metropolitan areas. Networking churches will grow to be regional clearinghouses for family services, possibly serving whole geographic regions. They will be home bases for smaller churches just beginning to offer family life ministries.

The call for more sophisticated family ministry programs dictates that family ministers be knowledgeable about community relations. Family ministers in networking models will need to be comfortable moving in secular and religious spheres. They will need to be well

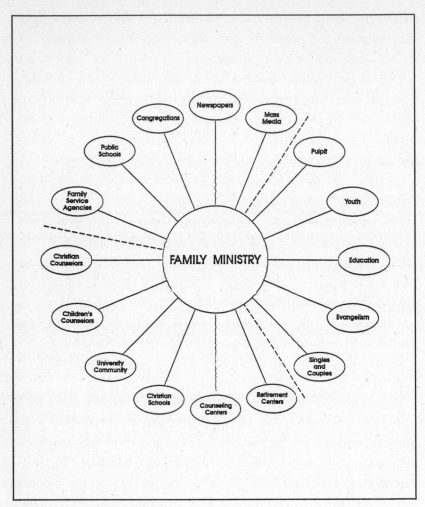

Fig. 6.12. Networking model

versed in business, medicine, public service, politics, and academics as they interact with civic leaders.

The opportunities for leadership and growth for aggressive networking churches are tremendous. Cities and communities are silently waiting for some agency or program to step into the gap and bring the many facets of family services together. The local church is in the ideal position to serve in that capacity with visionary leadership, competent family life ministers, and a passion for community ministry.

Results from the Models

What results can a church expect from an implementation of the models presented in this chapter? A church can expect many tangible and intangible results from a commitment to family ministry:

- The church will become a more edifying body, learning to minister to its own in crises.
- The church will empower families of all types to build family strengths and raise up children with the necessary skills to establish Christian homes.
- The community around the church will come to see the congregation as a group of people interested in more than their own self-preservation and agenda.
- Lost people will come to view Jesus as the Great Physician and ultimate source of authority and relational healing.
- The church will begin to address the issues of the culture through a Christian perspective rather than avoid the issues or remain silent.
- The church will be seen as a resource center.
- Staff unity and cooperation will be prioritized.
- Personal and familial spirituality will be stimulated and encouraged.
- Unchurched people will be drawn to the church through a variety of programs, groups, and relationships made in connection with this ministry.
- Many Christians, whose talents may have been unnoticed, will be used in their God-given roles.
- Church leaders will be able to move into a more proactive stance in relation to the problems of contemporary families.

Conclusion

In this chapter we have looked at an eight-stage developmental model for building a family life ministry. We have applied that model to the church without a staff person, the church with a combination minister, and the church moving into a full-time ministry. In each situation, the steps for implementing a ministry remain basically the same.

We have seen several examples of family life ministries. A church can take basic steps working as a committee. We explored an example of a full family life ministry directed heavily toward outreach.

No model is perfect. As previously stated, each family life ministry will be different depending upon many dynamic factors. I hope these models will stimulate your thinking in terms of designing a sensible and effective family ministry in your church. As family ministry matures, so the models will change and mature. What is most important is this: every church, no matter how large or how small, can do something to minister to its families. The question is not one of expertise or resources; it is one of desire.

7

OUTREACH

I attended a meeting of the American Society for Training and Development with my doctoral advisor, Dr. Tom Eaves, in Dallas several years ago. The monthly program featured outstanding professional trainers sharing their approaches to educating adults in business and nonprofit environments.

Our presenter for the evening was a young man who made a tremendous impact on my thinking. He was the corporate training director for a well-known pizza chain. His job, roughly described, was to take untrained high-school and college students and teach them how to make a consistently excellent pizza. The motivation level and attention span of the people varied tremendously!

He shared how his company had tried numerous approaches to connecting with the young workforce. Lectures, training manuals, demonstrations, even reward incentive programs—nothing seemed to work.

One night, as he was watching a weekly television program, an idea struck him. His young employees could mimic verbatim many of the sketches on that program.

Inspired by the program, he demonstrated via video cartoons the correct way to make pizza. Tapes were distributed, and the managers loved it. Store productivity increased, and the workforce demonstrated greater skills.

The young man finished his presentation by introducing us to a new term—*edutainment*. Edutainment is the combination of education and entertainment. It uses the connecting power of humor, drama, media, and song to communicate powerful messages about any topic. In our case we will consider the connecting power of edutainment with the contemporary family.

The Case for Edutainment

I wrote my doctoral dissertation on effective lecturing to adult audiences. After seeing mountains of video, reviewing mounds of data, and doing months of research, I came down to two major findings. Presenters who are considered effective with adult audiences combine a high level of subject competence with a high level of enthusiasm and energy. In other words, they know their subject and connect with the audience in a way that engages the people. The presentation is both educational and entertaining.

Some may find this concept distasteful and object. I believe one of the most insulting offerings we can make to a holy God is to communicate the story of His work here on earth in a boring manner. The redemptive story of God through Christ is many things, but it is not boring! I believe it is both spiritually educational and entertaining.

By entertaining, I do not mean a flippant story to amuse. I am referring to conveying the message with a life relevant illustration that is familiar to the audience. Think of your favorite teachers. Is there not an aspect of their teaching that is entertaining? It connects rationally and emotionally.

I remember a college professor who taught the epistle of Galatians to undergraduates. He was a passionate man who loved Paul's message of grace. He would begin the lecture with his coat on, tie neatly pulled up, in complete composure. But as he spoke of God's infinite grace, his blood pressure would rise, a large vein would stick out on his forehead, his coat would come off, and the tie would go down. He was caught up in the message. Was it entertaining? Only in the sense that his passion was infectious. I will always love Galatians. But was it educational? Absolutely. We learned more from his classes than from any others.

Edutainment offers a new blend of the sacred with the secular. It does not seek to water down the message of Jesus Christ. It tries to deliver it in a manner palatable to the listener—especially the listener with very little background in religious teachings. How often have we seen well-known Christian speakers or teachers fail to connect with an unchurched audience simply because they lack the vocabulary and illustrations to understand what is going on in their culture?

Edutainment is a platter on which the main course of food can be served to the learners. It is a framework for placing the message into contemporary thought, metaphor, and image. Certainly, the balance can shift from the message to the medium, but there are inherent dangers in a rigorous commitment to methodologies that cease to connect with people. Both approaches are imbalanced.

Luke often reports that people were amazed at Christ's teachings because He did not speak as the scribes and the Pharisees. Jesus taught with authority. But He also connected with the people. He spoke of farm and field, home life and common tragedy. He spoke right out of the front page of the daily newspaper. I believe we would be more likely to find Him on "Larry King Live" than on a televangelist special on cable. Why? Because He was committed to connecting with people.

Why Edutainment Works

Edutainment works because the past two generations of this country have been raised in a media-rich environment. The boomers and the busters have grown accustomed to a continual barrage of music, video, television, arts, graphics, slides, brochures, billboards, and every other form of communication media imaginable.

These two generations were born with nursery music on. They can sing the theme song to "Gilligan's Island" with greater accuracy than their own high-school alma mater. They can recount the great adventures of Captain James T. Kirk with such precision at a dinner party that one would think they were on the mission. They remember a soft drink is "the choice of a new generation." They can connect Nike's "Just Do It" from commercials, billboards, T-shirts, and magazines with such sophistication that they can use the phrase in humor.

So what is the point? The point is, our media-rich age has produced adult learners and audiences capable of making sophisticated mental connections from seemingly unrelated stimuli. They are persuaded not only through words but also through music, video, television, and the performing arts.

Informal learning has moved to a multidimensional model that accesses what we see, hear, think, taste, and touch. A great deal of this shift is the result of the advertising and entertainment industries. Television and marketing firms have revolutionized the way people learn informally in our culture. Now, when I receive my copy of *Modern Drummer* magazine, it no longer has just text; it has records to listen to. My wife's magazines are filled with packets of the latest fragrance samples. My cassette tapes come with lively graphics, a storage case, and a pocket listener's guide. The CD of my favorite group contains a booklet describing the entire life history. And they all come with offers to purchase the definitive videocassette tape for only $19.95!

Do you remember your junior high class at Bible school? We

were taught by Brother Bannister who lined us up around the room on pews and read the lesson off a yellow tablet for forty-five minutes. Forget the dialogue; forget any visuals; forget the application. We were there to endure the book of Acts.

Too many people have similar memories of church. The very mention of the Bible or the biblical concept of the family seems an invitation to yawn. Many people have come to expect the text to be boring, and they want no part of it.

Edutainment works not because it waters down the Word of God with slick advertising slogans. Edutainment works not because it tries to entertain everyone and make everyone feel very good. Edutainment works because it seeks to connect the eternal Word of God with a pluralistic culture that assumes there is no connection whatsoever. It challenges Christian communicators to move out of their own vocabulary and symbolism and into the language of the culture they wish to reach.

Connecting with a culture is dangerous business. We must not lose sight of the goal in our fascination with the methodology. Our purpose is to restore people's relationships with their God and families. Our methods may employ current techniques and technologies, but the methods must constantly come under the scrutiny of Scripture.

Edutainment works because it connects with the learning styles of people in the pews. It connects because it takes advantage of the media-rich environment that the boomers and busters are accustomed to. And it works because, just as in Christ's time, it illustrates the eternal principles of God's Word in a way that far surpasses the lecture or speech.

Tools of the Trade

When I speak to audiences about the family, I find they have been influenced by two major sources. The first source is the family of origin. We are shaped in our marriages by our parents, brothers, and sisters. The second source is society. People tend to articulate major themes about the family as articulated by the times in which they live, which is only natural.

The communications industry has made a significant impact on our thinking about the American family experience. I categorize these messages in these ways:

- *Fantasy.* Imagine what it would be like to live by your own rules, to live family life as corrupt as the daytime soaps or the latest movie plot.
- *News.* Many news and news magazine formats uncover and address problems of family living. Very few offer any hope or constructive answers to the issues.
- *Comedy.* Standup comedy and sitcoms document the tragedy and failure of the American family experience. They offer nothing to address the root problem.
- *Values communication.* Occasionally, a motion picture, story, or video not only will address an issue but also will treat it with unusual insights into values and coping. These works are usually highly regarded but scarce in number.

The tools of the trade in an edutainment model include music, both Christian and secular, drama, video, poetry and prose, illustrations, and graphic design, to name only a few.

To see the extent to which the media address family themes, try this experiment. Sit in front of the television armed with remote control and notepad. Spend a couple of hours flipping through the channels and observe the story lines. How many address some personal or family concern? What are the messages? What are the options being considered and executed? What assumptions underlie the decisions? What is viewed as a successful outcome? How many people do you know who are struggling with the same problem?

Try the same experiment with the music you listen to (and especially the stations you don't listen to!). What are the songwriters saying? Are they looking at family life from the eyes of persons trapped with no viable answers to life? Do they sing of the hopeless depression that hangs over our inner cities?

Music and drama carry great cultural messages about the pain and accepted prescriptions of our society. Rather than categorically condemn what's happening and throw away the remote control, why couldn't we explore these messages with our people? Why couldn't we help them evaluate the choices made by movie couples in light of God's Word?

The power of media to influence our lives is dramatic. One man, whose marriage was recovering from an affair, told me that he couldn't watch any show, listen to any comedian, or engage in an extended discussion without some mention of extramarital sex. His healing process was being delayed because of the incessant negative messages he was hearing about the acceptability of affairs. We can choose to dismiss the media messages, we can ignore them and hope they go away, or we can help people interpret the cultural messages they are hearing and ask them to evaluate them in light of their own experience and God's Word. The latter seems to hold great promise as we try to connect with struggling families.

An Example from *12 Angry Men*

Most family life ministers will spend a great deal of time assisting couples and families as they work through conflict. The lack of interpersonal conflict negotiation skills in churches is due to a large extent to the false assumption that all conflict is inherently evil.

While teaching a graduate course in interpersonal relations, I ran across a teacher's hint buried in the footnotes of the instructor's manual. It suggested the classic film *12 Angry Men*, starring young

Henry Fonda, as an excellent teaching tool to illustrate the concepts of interpersonal conflict resolution from a Christian viewpoint.

Being an old movie buff, I stopped by the video store and picked up the black-and-white film. Later that night, my wife was awakened to my laughter. When she came out from the bedroom, I informed her that I had found a movie documenting what church business meetings were like!

From that beginning we constructed a twelve-hour training seminar for church members based on the film. We used the entire film to train husbands and wives in listening skills, communication techniques, argumentation levels, and the power of effective Christian leadership.

The response was so powerful that church leaders began asking for the training to help them negotiate their leadership log jams. They saw themselves in the film, just as I had seen myself that first night in my living room. Corporate managers approached us because the training related so closely to the problems they were experiencing on the job with employees and managers.

Why did the mode of training work? Couldn't we have told people the principles in a third of the time? Couldn't we have given them a notebook with all the answers or blanks to fill in? Couldn't we have provided a motivational speaker? We could have done all of those things, but we didn't for one good reason. They would not have produced any change! Years later I encounter people who have taken that training and report the changes that have occurred in their lives because of the impact of interpreted visual messages.

The family enrichment training, which used the edutainment model, connected with people for several important reasons.

People were able to experience vicariously the emotional impact of the roles taken in the conflict.

It is one thing to state a principle or suggestion on paper. It is a different experience to see and feel how living that principle or making that suggestion affects people we are living and working with. The film experience brought people into contact with the materials.

People were consistently telling us that they saw themselves in the characters and the attitudes of the twelve men in that room. They saw the reactions they might give in a conflict situation and the impact that would have on the people around them.

It offered a lifelike feel and pace for the lessons.

One difficulty in teaching family relations skills is that the application of the principles comes during the hectic schedule of two or three busy lives. Concentrating on speaking kindly and offering positive feedback is fine, but doing those things while engaged in the harried demands of family life is a new challenge. The film allowed people to see principles applied in rough and approximated form and still be effective.

It offered a real-life role model.

Too much of what we see falls in the category of *"don't* do it like this." Families need real-life role models that they can approximate. The people in our training were able to see a man lead a group, practice honesty and integrity, and deal with his own emotions and anger. He was not perfect, but he was trying. It offered hope that we do not have to be as perfect as some family experts appear to be.

The use of an edutainment model in this framework offered powerful testimony to placing eternal principles into contemporary frameworks. Adult learners were able to identify problems, evaluate behavior alternatives, and experience the consequences of those selections. The entertainment aspect of the training added a real-life dimension to the experience that would have been missing from traditional educational approaches. The text was amplified and explained in real-life terms. Paul's command to honor one another was seen as well as heard.

Guess Who's Coming to Dinner?

As I developed the concept of edutainment, I became convinced that it was a natural avenue for addressing community guests on their own turf. When I could draw from their music, programs, and media-relevant messages and then interpret them with God's purpose in mind, I felt people would listen and learn.

While teaching family relations in a community college, I consistently asked my students what role religion played in their families. The responses were quite candid: "Our family was very religious when I was growing up. My mom and dad made sure we all went to church and Sunday school. After my wife and I married, we meant to go to church but never really got into the habit. We really need to and I think we would, you know, if we could find a church family that seemed to really care about us and our family."

They represented two general streams of thought. The first was that no church was really interested in them. Churches existed for those inside the four walls, not the people on the street. The agenda was for the saints, not the sinners. The second was, I believe, an outgrowth of the first. They viewed Christianity as a personal commitment separate from organized religion.

Yet as we discussed marriage, parenting, sexuality, and money from a Christian perspective, the students warmed to the idea that perhaps the Bible did have something relevant and authoritative to say to their lives. Students would often bring their spouses to the sessions just to listen in. Many would remark, "I wish I had learned this years ago." When the veil of mystery surrounding the text was brought down in a nonthreatening environment, the power of Christ's words to address human needs was once again felt.

Close to the end of the final semester of teaching, I conducted an informal survey. I asked my students to tell me if they were given two tickets to a dinner theater where the topics we had discussed in class were addressed in an edutainment format, would they attend with their spouses? Thirty-nine out of forty answered affirmatively. When quizzed whether they would attend if the theater were sponsored by a church, they unanimously agreed. They would be delighted to know of a church that cared about ministering to families.

Our first task was to create a dinner theater environment that would address contemporary family themes from a Christian context. The programs used a variety of formats including music, drama, dialogue, video, and slides. The issues were presented along with biblically based solutions. Guests were invited to attend a more educationally based seminar at the church following the theater. The approach raised family problems from a cultural perspective and then addressed them from God's Word.

A Quick Review

Community outreach through an edutainment model includes a combination of contemporary media and methods, an examination of relevant family themes, and an exploration of God's Word on the topic. It capitalizes on the various learning styles of the adult audience. It assumes there are barriers between the church and the community and attempts to build bridges between them. It capitalizes on our media-rich environment, informal learning systems, and ability to form cognitive structures from a multitude of structures. It presents the eternal message on a contemporary platter but holds the methodology accountable through spiritual discernment of God's Word.

Family ministry as an outreach tool requires a unique set of values and a special heart for ministry. The church that readily values an internal family life ministry may struggle when it considers reaching the community. It is not a question of methodology. It is a question of the heart. Does the church have the heart and values for reaching the community?

Do We Have a Heart for Reaching the Community?

What do you suppose the disciples were thinking as they descended that hill from the Samaritan well and entered the village? Were they thrilled at the prospects of entering a village that would be open to Jesus? Or were they concerned that perhaps the "outreach thing" had been taken a little too far? Maybe, as their heels dug into the rough stones descending from the well, they would have liked to turn the other direction.

Effective outreach does not begin with actions or methods. It is a heart question. It is a question of values. How much do we really care about lost and suffering people in the world around us? God cared so much that He chose to redeem this broken experiment called humankind with His Son. Many give lip service to caring, but their hearts are reluctant. They are fine up on the hill by the well. There they can look over the village in reclusive comfort. Let those in need come up here. But when they descend the hill, outreach begins to look a lot more threatening.

Effective outreach through family life ministry is built on the answers to ten major questions:

1. Am I willing to sit by the wells and listen?
2. Am I willing to suspend judgment long enough to hear the pain in people's lives?
3. Am I willing to listen to their world messages through the

media long enough to learn how they are struggling and reinterpret with meaning and relevance?

4. Am I willing to admit that I may be initially viewed at best as irrelevant and at worst as hostile?

5. Am I willing to be faced with many people who may not fit neatly into the boxes I have for my ministry?

6. Am I secure enough as a person to be used, abused, and hurt by people I don't know very well?

7. Am I willing to be misunderstood from within the camp at times because I work with people outside the camp?

8. Am I willing to be a family spokesperson for the community within my church?

9. Am I willing to gently and persistently pursue change in structures and procedures that may prevent lost persons from gaining access to my church very easily?

10. Am I willing to experience tragic defeat and incredible victory?

The answers to these questions will say a great deal about the values of the minister and the church considering outreach through family ministry. I believe a significant value shift will be necessary for most churches to move from an internally based family life ministry to an outreach model. Naively assuming that valuing ministry to the congregation means valuing ministry to the community is a dangerous assumption. Many churches that welcome an internal family life ministry are poorly equipped to minister outside their four walls.

My experience has been that most established churches give lip service to the theory of outreach but little real practice. They may offer some outreach programs, but they are packaged and tailored for believers or individuals who are Christian friendly. They are not willing to move beyond the rites and traditions of their religious custom to meet community people where they live. As a result, they play elaborate games of denial and congratulate themselves for minuscule successes in bringing very few people into outreach-oriented programming.

This need for a values shift was demonstrated a decade ago with the introduction of the James Dobson Focus on the Family film series. Churches that had once never attracted visitors from the community suddenly discovered something. In many cases, by sheer accident, they scheduled the film series and put it on their marquees. Visitors flocked into the foyers, down the main aisles, and sat front and center every night. Why? Because their needs were being met. When they are in enough pain, people will go through any barrier—even a religious one—to get relief.

The outreach question, for many churches, will call for a dramatic shift in values. Even churches that have experienced success with programming shifts, such as the Dobson film series and other events, will balk at values shifts because they represent an alteration in the basic fabric of the church.

To put it candidly, many churches have been built a little south of the well. They want to be in the community with a good location but not too close to the real problems. They don't want to get close to the wells of people's problems. It is one thing to preach about family problems; it is a whole different matter to minister to family problems.

Many churches, like the disciples, will go down the hill toward the village with their heels reluctantly dug into the rock. They do not want to be there, and they resent the family minister's efforts to push them in that direction. Without addressing the values question the minister may find the people running south for Jerusalem and the program at the bottom of the well.

The Community That Is Ready to Join Hands

One of the most exciting opportunities in family life ministry is the chance to interact with the business and professional communities. Many businessmen and businesswomen are open to working with a family life ministry in their place of employment.

We recently completed a series of lessons entitled "Living by Personal Mission." One businessman who owned his own firm told me, "We could use anything taught in this series with my employees. The things you are addressing here at church are exactly the same things I am struggling with in my place of business." What a refreshing change! No longer are spiritual things being viewed as separate and disjointed from real life. The integration is obvious to business-people.

While completing my doctoral internship, I worked with the professional education division of one of the "big eight" accounting firms. I was asked to conduct a training needs analysis of administrative support staff to determine what kinds of training they would benefit from. Although technical training was needed in areas such as word processing, computing, and so on, the areas of interpersonal relations ranked highest on the list. People needed people-relating skills.

I learned from interviews with managers, and from subsequent conversations with businesspeople, that family problems dramatically affect the workplace. Think of the time lost as a man or woman struggles through the legal procedures of a divorce. Consider the productivity that is lost when managers and employees cannot get along and work together.

These issues, and a host of others, can trace their roots to the same lack of skills that family life ministry addresses. One of the great untapped mission areas in the world today is corporate America. Family life ministry is a natural avenue to offer training and therapy to companies that might not be able to afford them.

I have worked for several years with one businessman in Atlanta. He invites me to address his employees each year about personal mission and interpersonal relations. He has set up a fund to help his company families afford counseling at our center. He has defined a set of business practice ethics for his employees that describes appropriate behavior. He is trying to build a corporate environment that exudes interpersonal health.

Family life ministry, when it joins hands with the business community, helps the local church be perceived as a group of people who are genuinely concerned.

The opportunities for integrating with the community through business are enormous. It may be through training in corporate environments. It may be through offering low-cost counseling. It may be through networking with helping professions such as doctors, coun-

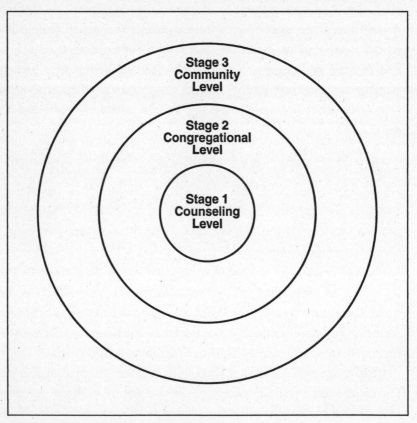

Fig. 7.1. Connecting ministry to the community

selors, Realtors, and local governments. It may be through offering a free site to support groups in the area. The opportunities are endless if one has a heart for ministry and a creative mind.

A Connecting Model

A church that is interested in connecting family life ministry with the community may begin with an internal family ministry and expand to the surrounding neighborhood. I propose a three-stage model of development (see fig. 7.1). The first stage builds a backstop of counseling and referral sources to assist families having problems. The second stage focuses on an internal family life ministry within the local congregation. The third stage expands the offerings to the community at large.

The counseling level might include therapy, support groups, local networks, and referral sources. The program within the local church should be built around a developmental faith in families curriculum. In other words, the ministry should address the needs of children, youths, and families at each phase of the developmental life cycle. To do this, the family life minister would seek to implement an age-appropriate family life curriculum at each stage of the life cycle. (See fig. 7.2.)

Once the foundation has been laid by building a counseling ministry and an internal program, the next step is to move into local outreach. This involves asking connecting questions: How do we connect with our culture? How do we connect with people's struggles and family needs? How do we connect them with the eternal Word of God in a relevant way? How do we connect them with Jesus Christ and His grace?

This model uses five levels of connecting in terms of Stage 3 outreach into the community. Each level proposes a challenge that outreach family life ministry must address (see fig. 7.3).

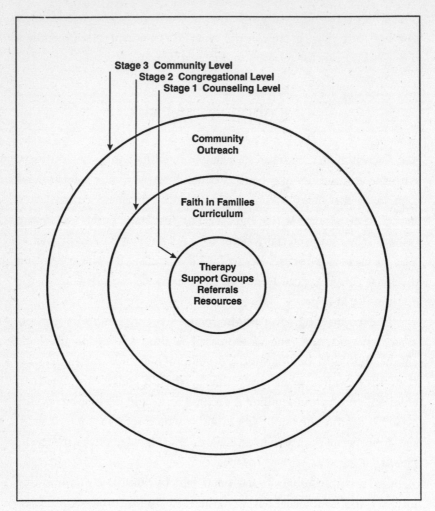

Fig. 7.2. Programs of connection

Level 1: Connected in Culture, Communications, and Climate

This is the beginning point. The outreach family life ministry must listen at the wells to gain an understanding of the culture and communications of the people it is trying to reach. Too often we dive into programs without asking who we are trying to contact.

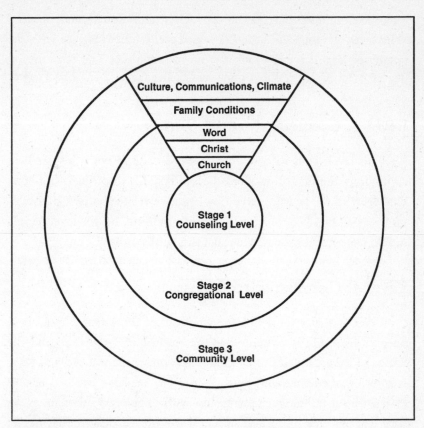

Fig. 7.3. Five levels of outreach

Climate refers to the ability of the ministry to create a nonthreatening atmosphere for the target audience. Time must be spent at this level understanding the nature and function of the culture. The community response on this level would ideally be, "I didn't know anyone would listen to my concerns."

Level 2: Connected to Family Conditions

Once again we ask questions of needs analysis: What are community families struggling with? How are they the same or different from other families in this church? What unique problems are not addressed by government agencies, other churches, or helping professionals? Where can we minister to the needs of community families with the unique gifts we have as God's people in this place? The response on this level should be, "I didn't know you cared enough to understand."

Level 3: Connected to the Word

This level seeks to connect the Word of God with the needs of community families. How does the Word speak to problems of conflict, drug abuse, and poverty? How can we relate the text in a relevant way to family problems of the community? In this level people should respond, "I didn't know that was in the Bible."

Level 4: Connected to Christ

Level 4 brings Christ to the forefront as the Great Physician in people's lives. He is presented as the Author of family life and the Savior of unredeemed humankind. He is presented as Lord and King worthy of obedience and faith. Too often, we have jumped to this level without building a relationship with people. At other times we have left out this important step and ministered only to felt needs. The presentation of Jesus Christ as Lord is a natural part of a holistic family life ministry. The natural response should be, "I didn't know Christ cared so much for me."

Level 5: Connected to the Body

The final level presents the challenge of integrating the new child of God into the faith family. Note we have moved from Stage 1 into Stage 2, which is the church. Often it is impossible to move people who have been reached through family ministry into the body of Christ. This may be due to unhealthy patterns of belief and practice within the church. That is why the family life minister must address questions of values and build a healthy faith family within the local church before effective outreach can begin. The response on this level would be, "I didn't know any church could care this much and feel like my home!"

Let's return to Stage 1, and discuss the relationship of counseling to an outreach model. In this process, lines of referral will develop from each level of the outreach program and from within the local congregation. In simple terms, as we connect with the community, discuss their needs, look at the text relevantly, and look toward Jesus Christ, we will uncover therapeutic needs. As these needs surface, they can be referred to a counseling ministry for direct help. (See fig. 7.4.)

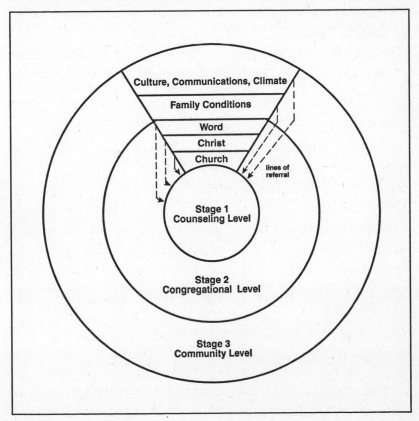

Fig. 7.4. Lines of referral

So our model becomes an integrated one. It demonstrates the holistic nature of family ministry and the holistic nature of the ministry of Jesus Christ. It offers

- multiple entry points for unbelievers.
- a realistic approach to family life problems from a biblical perspective.
- an opportunity for members to use their unique gifts in service and outreach.
- a logical way for people to move from a position of ministry through felt needs to active participation in the body of Christ.
- immediate opportunities to have counseling needs met in a confidential manner.
- a deeper understanding of how God in Christ has intended the individual, family, church, and community to work together in harmony.

What Programs Can Be Integrated into the Model?

Most churches will develop programs to include in the model I have just shared. We have discussed at length the offerings that could be developed in a counseling ministry. Let's consider some offerings that you might develop for an internal program or community outreach purposes.

Searchers' Bible Class

Devote one adult Bible class to a scriptural-relational study of the text. Apply biblical principles to family relationships. Study a gospel with an eye toward marriage, parenting, communications, or ethics. This class could be offered on-site in a traditional Bible class arrangement or off-site in a hotel or restaurant. It would specifically target Levels 3 and 4 in our model.

Community Enrichment Series

One of the most popular programs we have offered has been our community enrichment program. Taking some of the most relevant family issues of the day, we address them from a Christian standpoint in a class designed specifically for guests. Advertising is done in the local neighborhood as a part of the church's effort to build a good neighbor image. Newcomers to the class are given complete anonymity but receive additional mailers concerning other family life events.

Some churches that have altered their Sunday night formats to offer community outreach programs have met with great success. They may do this on a monthly or quarterly basis. It is an excellent forum for lectures, panel discussions, films, and special dramatic presentations.

Family Life Series

Consider establishing a series each year that focuses on family needs. One speaker may address a major theme, or many speakers in a family life conference may address the unique needs of specialized family forms. Build a tradition that is a regular part of the church calendar.

Family Network Newsletters/Mailers

Family life ministry newsletters can be sent to members and community guests to update them on events and opportunities. They can disseminate information on a family issue or review a relevant book. If they are well done, they can be useful outreach tools to remind visitors that they might want to return to church for another class or seminar.

Special Seminars

Many educational seminars would be an excellent outreach into the community. A church close to a university might offer a premarital retreat in the spring of each year. A church in a growing section of the community might emphasize parenting or a financial planning ministry. A church in an older, more established area might sponsor a health fair or grandparenting seminar. The options are limitless based on the needs of the community and the creativity of the ministry.

Tape Ministries

With so many commuters listening to tapes, almost any church could develop a highly successful outreach tape ministry by providing resources to nonmembers. Perhaps the ministry might establish a tape club to supply a family enrichment tape to each member on a monthly basis. The listeners would receive useful information along with invitations to attend follow-up seminars at the church. High-quality presentation and packaging would be essential. The church would once again build the reputation for being a church that cares about people.

Preventive Classes

The developmental faith in families curriculum I have talked of could include topics on a range of family life subjects:

- Spouse selection
- Parenting young children
- Parenting teens
- The empty nest
- Marital communications

- Marriage enrichment
- Financial management
- Time management
- Building spiritual values in the home
- Depression
- Christian business ethics
- Preparing for adolescence
- Building spiritual traditions
- Divorce
- Single parenting
- Human sexuality
- Death, dying, and grief
- Dealing with illness
- AIDS
- CPR
- Affair prevention
- Job loss
- Alcohol and drug abuse
- Conflict resolution skills
- Blended families
- Singles
- Helping aging parents

Marriage Camp and Family Retreats

Productive marriage and family enrichment traditions include weekend retreats and family vacations. Enrichment of any form is designed for persons with reasonably healthy family relationships. It is not a substitute for therapy. Marriage camp is a yearly couples enrichment program we have offered for couples at various stages in their married life. Family retreats encourage families to build relationships and strengthen spiritual ties. Both offer an outlet for building relationships in the community.

Engaged Couples Ministry

Most churches and communities would benefit from a comprehensive premarital counseling program offered by the local church. The program would give members and nonmembers a chance to evaluate their upcoming marriages in light of current research and biblical counsel. Two tracks could be offered: one for those marrying for the first time, and a second for those remarrying and forming blended families. There are many excellent tools to draw from in premarital work, such as the Taylor-Johnson Temperament Analysis and the Prepare Inventory.

Video Resources

With the advent of the videotape industry, family life ministry should capitalize on education brought into the living room. Since many families cocoon on the weekends, topics could be addressed in the privacy of the home. Videos could be produced and distributed to guests. Professionally produced tapes could be bought and distributed or checked out for use by the community.

Many other courses could be offered that would directly address the needs of families. These might be taught by in-house resource people or guest speakers. Some could be addressed through prepared educational curricula purchased off the shelf.

How Can You Make Offerings Guest Friendly?

Many churches select topics and speakers to reach the community and then shoot themselves in the foot by not paying enough attention to the details that screen out community guests. I suggest the following checklist to build a community class that is guest friendly:

- Select a time and place conducive to guests brought by members.
- Select a location that provides immediate access in and out of the building.
- Select a topic that is appealing to the community, and give it an interesting name. If it's a series, use intriguing subtitles.
- Keep in mind the time of year and the audience you are trying to attract.
- Recruit and train class hosts who are skilled at being attentive to guests without hovering over them.
- Recruit and train a class host and hostess who welcome the class and serve as contact persons to the community visitors.
- Build a philosophy of guest comfort. If something alienates them, change it.
- Keep in-house administration and announcements to a minimum.
- Provide well-produced handouts or materials for future reference. Have some family ministry information printed and available in the entry.
- Keep presentations upbeat, positive, and solution oriented.
- Use media every session but try not to duplicate from week to week.
- Try opening the class with a familiar video clip as people are arriving to capture attention and reduce anxiety.
- Advertise the series or topics in the community.
- Let films and videos augment the class, but build on the relationship of the teacher and the students.
- The person who welcomes the class should be relational and friendly. The teacher should be able to deliver the lesson in an informational and engaging way. Both should make it a habit to learn how to build bridges to nonmembers.
- Try using a case study or role play instead of a straight lecture style.

Excellent community outreach classes are conducted when a leadership team gives the appropriate attention to detail. It is much better to do fewer educational/outreach events and be able to do them well than to throw together classes just to have something to offer. When we offer something to people in the community, we should treat them as if they were honored guests in our home—with dignity, courtesy, and respect. The dividends to the kingdom cannot be measured by an attitude like this.

They Understood the Times

During the final days of the wilderness period of David's life, he was encamped at Hebron. He was banished from the presence of Saul. He and his ragtag band of outlaws had been run up and down the countryside fleeing from the king's men. Memories of his anointing as future king and the face of his best friend Jonathan were but faded memories in the jigsaw puzzle called his life.

Then one day, the chronicler records, history was changed forever. Perhaps that morning David scanned the horizon like any good general would do. Much to his surprise he saw some men on the horizon. Then their numbers began to grow—dozens, hundreds, thousands! More men than he could count. Could it be the end? Did Saul hire mercenaries to drive him into the ground?

The multitude of fighting men surrounded the camp and began to march in. The tension mounted as David soon realized they were the core members of Saul's army. He even saw Saul's relatives and family members! But David could not spot Saul. Finally, the huge gathering stood before him and his small band of followers.

Then came the announcement: "We have come to make you king!" Thousands upon thousands of fighting men volunteered to serve in the ranks of David's army because they respected his integrity and commitment to God. Kinsmen from Saul's tribe of

Benjamin who could shoot the bow or sling stones with either hand came. Strong warriors volunteered. Three thousand of Saul's kinsmen stepped across the lines that day to pledge loyalty to David.

But buried in the military march were the men of Issachar. In one of the most beautiful statements of the Old Testament the chronicler recorded, "The sons of Issachar . . . had understanding of the times, to know what Israel ought to do" (1 Chron. 12:32).

The men had the spiritual gift of discernment and wisdom. They understood the days called for decisive actions unknown in Israel's history. Never before had God's people had to abandon a head of state, but the time had come, and they were the men who called the shot.

We live in days that call for men and women to understand the times and know what to do. We live in times that call for tremendous wisdom to understand God's Word and apply it to an extensive catalog of family difficulties.

Churches need to step up to the challenge and minister to community families. The effort will demand time, money, and personnel. But the most serious shift will be in terms of values. We will, like the men of Issachar, have to rethink the assumptions we were brought up to accept. For the family life minister open to reevaluating assumptions, the well can be deep and filled with fruitful opportunities to minister.

Conclusion

This chapter introduced the concepts regarding the implementation of a community outreach family life ministry. It explained edutainment as a workable solution to confront the barriers between the church and the community. Edutainment seeks to package the eternal message in contemporary life images, music, and drama. It capitalizes on the fact that the two major generations now heading families, the boomers and the busters, have been raised in a media-rich environment.

I have suggested a connecting model that integrates the three levels of family life ministry: counseling, internal family ministry, and external outreach. The model calls for connecting with community families and their struggles as we lead them to a connection with the heavenly Father and the body of Christ. Out of these connections will come opportunities for counseling and family services.

Programs connected to an outreach model will be unique in each church locale. Some churches will offer preventive classes; others, premarital counseling or support groups. Theater, retreats, publications, tape, and video offer opportunities for the church to network with the community and strengthen family ties. Each family ministry program should develop its approach based on the needs of neighborhood families.

But the underlying shift toward community outreach must be one of values. Too many ministries get bogged down in counseling-only outreach models and fail to build programs that proactively reach unchurched people. Normally, these are problems of values and assumptions. Outreach is not valued highly enough to produce the internal value shifts needed to produce effective outreach.

How important is it to constantly evaluate values? Luke records an expert in the law asking Jesus, "What must I do to inherit eternal life?" "Love the Lord your God with all your heart, and love your neighbor, too," affirmed the Master.

But the question "Who is my neighbor?" produced one of the most meaningful stories in all the Bible. The good Samaritan was the model of action-oriented faith that was willing to break out of the prescribed social roles to help a fellow human in need. Jesus' reply was profoundly simple. He did not tell the lawyer to debate about it. He did not tell him to reflect upon it. He told him to "go and do likewise" (Luke 10:25–37).

The coming years will produce churches that have the good Samaritan mentality. Churches will learn the joy of giving a cup of cold water in Jesus' name. And I believe we will once again see the reemergence of the people of Issachar who understand the times and know what to do.

8

DEVELOPING A SIXTH SENSE

When I was a little boy my mother bought me a big picture book of Native Americans. My favorite picture was a group of braves standing at a waterfall with nets trying to catch trout as they went over the falls. It looked like great fun.

Today many church leaders stand at the waterfalls with nets trying to salvage something of marriages or families that are self-destructing. We catch a few. Most go right on by or through our nets.

It makes more sense to go upstream to the fork in the river and put up a sign: "Don't come this way. There are rapids down here. You're headed for the falls and we may not be able to help you."

Churches today are in an ideal stance to put up signs at the bends in the river. We can point people to God's plan for the family. We can warn them of the white water ahead. We can prepare them for the changes to come in their family life and offer guidance when they struggle in the rapids.

Family ministry is about change. The family life minister is in the business of managing a change process. You help unhealthy families learn more effective ways of dealing with their problems. You address the needs of healthy families as they prepare for crises along the life cycle. You help community families gain a deeper trust in the local church as a viable agent of ministry. You assist church leaders in carving out more effective rules for the family of faith to live by. In all of these functions, you act as a change agent.

The turnover rate of ministers in American churches is well documented. Yet some people are able to land in a church and minister effectively regardless of the circumstances. In some cases they may not match well the congregation or the community. Why are these individuals able to function so effectively?

I believe they have developed a sixth sense. It is the ability to parachute into new and unfamiliar territory, get a feel for the lay of the land, and then move toward the most appropriate targets.

Some ministers have a natural feel for this process. But many men and women have been lost because there was not an effective road map to alert them to approaching dangers.

In this chapter we will discuss how changes occur on five levels of ministry functioning. Family life ministry presents some unique challenges to the minister that are not found in pulpit, youth, or educational work. If you can cultivate a sixth sense, ministering to families can be a rewarding process as people slowly grow in spiritual and familial maturity.

The Five Levels of Sixth Sense

As the family life minister, you will operate on at least five levels of personal, ministerial, and organizational complexity within a local

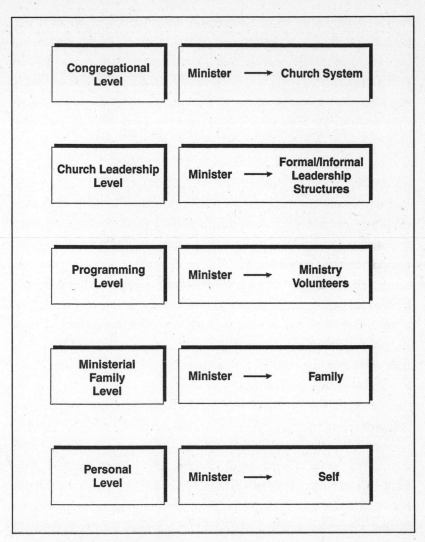

Fig. 8.1. Levels in a local church

church. Change constantly occurs on all five levels and must be managed appropriately. A shift in one level will send ripple effects to a different level. A change in one area will affect all the others. (See fig. 8.1.)

The congregational level refers to your relationship and that of the ministry to the church at large. The church leadership level refers to your relationship to all formal and informal leadership structures in the local church, including staff, elders, deacons, boards, and standing committees. The programming level encompasses people serving within the ministry and people served by the ministry. Your spouse and family are key ingredients to the success or failure of the family ministry and are represented by a separate level. Finally, you must consider your personality, skills, temperament, and background as you manage the change process.

In family ministry these five levels are in a constant state of fluctuation. Family life ministers who have developed a keen sixth sense can gauge what is happening on each level at all times. They select and implement appropriate changes with a sense of timing that does not disrupt the entire system.

Some family life ministers become discouraged because they land in a congregation, assess the needs to be great, and attempt to go in fifteen different directions at once. Others implement changes in the programming, leadership, or congregational levels without regard for building credibility and trust.

Let's examine each level.

The Personal Level

Do I understand who I am as a person and how that affects me in the ministry? The first area of awareness that you must gain is an ongoing understanding of your internal wiring. The more you understand about yourself, your temperament, family of origin, background, and work styles, the better. Too many people enter and leave the ministry wounded because they have not endeavored to understand who they are and what are their strengths and weaknesses.

This need was brought home to me graphically very early in my ministry career. Several businessmen came to me with a job opportunity to begin a chain of high-quality family-based day care centers.

Before we proceeded with the plans, they insisted that I receive an aptitude profile at the Johnson-O'Conner Institute in Irving, Texas. The two-day evaluation was priceless. I learned that I had a subjective personality, which meant whenever I worked on something, I liked to leave my unique stamp on it. That one piece of information has helped me immensely in understanding the way I work as a minister and how I relate as a part of a multiple staff.

Too many people enter the ministry without spending one hour in understanding their personality and temperament. Check the ministerial dropout statistics. They may reflect the result of too little self-evaluation before the commitment to ministry is made.

No one is perfect. We all approach the task of ministry with a unique set of glasses on. The responsible thing to do is to occasionally take off those glasses and look at the lenses. The irresponsible thing to do is to deny that we are wearing them at all.

Personal counseling is a useful and necessary tool for survival in modern ministry. The stresses and expectations are so great that a minister needs a trusted relationship where doubts, fears, and alternatives can be discussed. It may be with a pastoral counselor. A small group of responsible friends may serve as a support group. This should be seen not as a weakness but as a sincere attempt to recharge the ministerial battery.

The need for deeper self-awareness is especially important for the family life minister. Most graduate training programs in marriage and family therapy require this as a part of the formal training process. Family ministers who enter the field from other avenues will want to consider the significance of this step in their development.

Can I set and maintain appropriate personal and family boundaries? If you are unwilling to set personal and family boundaries, you will be quickly consumed. You must learn your limits and set your pace. The cold reality is, there will never be enough time, and there will always be one more thing to do.

Maintaining personal boundaries includes setting time for personal refreshment and renewal. One of the first things that flies out the window in a busy schedule is a reading program. Because you must keep up to date in several fields, a reading program is essential if you are to stay on the cutting edge.

Screen and refer counseling cases that are beyond your area of expertise. Too many ministers counsel far beyond their area of expertise. They are frustrated, and the counseling cases are not helped efficiently. Everyone loses when the family minister does not set appropriate counseling boundaries.

Learn to say no to demands and opportunities that may be very good and proper. Most ministerial demands are worthy. You do not choose between things that are good and bad; you choose between better and best. There are so many family problems and so many good works that could be done. Learn to be selective.

That includes learning to say no to people who expect very high standards. Some church leaders who promise to protect and defend the minister's time and energy are often the ones who ask the minister to violate personal or professional boundaries as a favor to them. Setting appropriate boundaries with these people is essential—but often difficult.

Boundary setting is a healthy thing for you to do. It is an ongoing process that is facilitated by an open working relationship with the leaders of the church.

Do I maintain the highest level of professional ethics? You must set an example of the highest level of ministerial and personal ethics. There is a growing need to rebuild the reputation of ministers as credible helpers, and you must be on the front line of this battle.

First, you must maintain a spotless reputation in the area of sexual relationships. Precautions should be taken to build and maintain appropriate boundaries. Clear communications should take place between you and the leaders concerning these issues at the initiation and throughout the course of the ministry.

It is inexcusable for a minister to use a position of leadership in the church to exploit members sexually. Furthermore, it is inexcusable for congregations to deny these problems.

Second, you must maintain appropriate ethics in regard to confidentiality. We have talked at length in this book about the need for confidentiality in the local church. You will learn many things about many church families. You must hold this information in the strictest professional confidence. It is a violation of professional ethics to use case stories and illustrations without the consent of persons involved. Conversations, whether public or private, that reveal information communicated in a confidential way are always inappropriate.

Third, you owe it to yourself and the congregation to pursue continuing education. This ministerial rebirth is essential to meet the changing needs of congregational families.

You are in several worlds all at once. You must be a therapist with a broad range of expertise. You must be an educator of children, youths, and adults. You must be a lecturer and speaker. You must be able to do competent research and writing. All these skills require constant upgrading. Most churches allow for some time devoted to continuing education but never enough. Wise is the minister who learns to develop a plan of continuing education through tapes, reading, video, and personal study to stay fresh in the field.

One of the most enjoyable shifts I have made in my training has been away from attending only organized conferences and toward studying under what I call content experts. Several years ago, I decided I wanted to upgrade my preaching skills. Instead of reading more books, attending a conference, or listening to more tapes, I decided to find a content expert. I offered to "buy" a day of an excellent preacher's time. We made a contract where I sent him tapes and samples ahead of time of my preaching, and he supplied me with resources to read and listen to before our day together. We had a highly productive day of intensive downloading where my skills were improved directly and dramatically. My content expert was delighted to work one on one with a serious learner, and a close personal relationship developed that has lasted for years.

One final area of personal development as it affects the change process is authenticity. Many competencies and skills are vital for you to master. But this characteristic stands above all the others. Your ability to be perceived by the church and your peers as an authentic Christian leader is critical to your effectiveness.

Authenticity, integrity, and self-discipline are nonnegotiable in the development of the family life minister. Families are hungry to see role models. You can be a part of the role modeling for the local church. But you must embody the characteristics of love, patience, discipline, integrity, and honesty before you can teach them.

I am not calling for gold-plated, clinical-talking ministers. I am speaking of men and women who walk the streets of our cities and towns and come back to instruct us on the reality of the Christian faith in the complexity of daily living. A powerful family ministry embodies the marvelous simplicity of the ministry of Jesus Christ: "Those who are well have no need of a physician, but those who are sick. . . . I did not come to call the righteous, but sinners, to repentance" (Matt. 9:12–13).

The Ministerial Family Level

The second level of sixth sense that you must constantly evaluate is your family. Recent studies indicate that the level of dissatisfaction among ministry families is so high that ministry is seen as a threat to healthy family life. Ministers, spouses, and children report growing disillusionment with local church work. When asked how they plan on caring for their ministerial families, many church leaders look stunned as if it is the first time they have ever considered the question.

Whole books have been written on the subject of the ministerial family. It is not my purpose to duplicate that material here. I would like to address some of the specific questions that you must ask yourself with regard to your family life.

How do my spouse and I work together as a ministerial team? Probably no role places you and your family in the proverbial fishbowl with more regularity than the role of the family life minister. You'll hear, "You aren't supposed to have family problems. You're the family minister!" The pressures on the spouse and children can be unrealistic and intolerable if the two people do not work together as a ministerial team.

When we first entered ministry, I made a deal with my wife, Jennifer. I understood that the pressures would be great on her, and at times she might have a hard time making me understand what she was going through. I gave her an undated resignation letter in a sealed envelope and told her that if the pressures of ministry ever became intolerable or threatened our relationship, she had the right to pull out my resignation letter and ask me to use it! Thankfully, our communication has always been open enough to talk through problems.

Your first priority in building a ministry is to your family. Your spouse and children should get prime time, not leftovers. They should see you set boundaries to allow time to be with your family and friends.

Ministerial couples may face many tough economic demands. I believe the dual-career working couple in ministry is cut with a two-edged sword. The church may not be able to afford to support the minister, yet members may often look down on the working wife because she is not the unpaid traditional ministerial wife they have grown accustomed to. Guilt, anger, and disillusionment can be deposited in deep wells of resentment within the marriage. Church leaders must learn to affirm the working ministerial marriage and help support ministry marriages. I have found that most churches do not, and it is the minister's job to set a first line of defense.

Ministry couples need to relearn how to have fun. Family life ministry can be very grim. It involves a great deal of grief work, and all too often the fruits of our labors are not seen. The family life minister needs a life outside ministry, and I believe it must center on the marriage.

I remember one of the most embarrassing moments in our marriage. We had been in ministry a short time, both of us were working, and I was attending graduate school. We had been unable to afford a family vacation to our favorite spot at the beach for several summers. Finally, we saved all year and left town and telephone behind. We couldn't wait to get away.

About midweek it began raining. My wife and daughter decided to cozy up to a movie in the room, and I decided to take a run in the rain on the beach. The beach was deserted as I headed out. Far in the distance I could see some people fishing in the surf. As I ran by, I heard a familiar voice, and someone called out, "Brother Don!" Three of our church members were fishing by themselves in the middle of nowhere. One said, "Say, we're going down to this little church tonight. Can you go with us? They don't have a preacher, and they really could use a guy like you to fill in for them!" Needless to say, my wife was not excited to learn that we had saved up all year just so I could go back to work. At that time I did not have the discipline to say no.

You and your spouse must work together as a team. You must develop excellent communication skills. You must learn to calendar time commitments together. You must learn to look ahead at each year and determine what you want to accomplish in the ministry, in your marriage, and in your relationship with your children. If you, as a couple, learn to balance the demands of ministry and family, family life ministry can be one of the most rewarding areas of church work.

Do I respect the privacy of my family? One of my favorite cartoons pictures a preacher walking into the nursery to look at his new baby boy. With great pride he asks, "And how is my little bundle of sermon illustrations this morning?"

Too many preachers' kids can identify with the glass house syndrome because they have been the closing illustrations for sermons, teachers' appreciation banquets, and parenting seminars. Just once they would like to get their hands on the microphone and have equal time to tell a few stories on their parents.

Because you work in family life, it is natural for you to draw on the events in the life of your family. These stories are often priceless and can add validity and humanness to the ministry. However, if you share stories and events about the family without consent, you are infringing upon their rights to privacy.

I made a deal with my wife early on in my work as a family life minister. I told her that I would share stories and illustrations from our relationship only with her prior permission. I did not want her out in the audience worrying each time I illustrated a point. I have the same arrangement with my children and my students. Some of my most poignant stories have been shared by my students in college courses, but I will repeat them only when I have their permission. This may seem like a small point, but it builds credibility and trust between the minister and the family.

Do I protect my family from people who would threaten them? A sad reality of ministerial life is that there are people who would intentionally damage our families. Their attitudes and actions prove that they cannot be trusted near our spouses and children. You must, at times, be a buffer between your family and these individuals.

I remember one person who could not accept people who did not fit into her mold. Her dislike of people who had anything to do with divorce was so acute that she could not even be civil to them.

My wife has been married before. It was a horrible situation that ended in divorce even though every effort was made to salvage the relationship. Since I, as a family life minister worked with divorced and remarried families, I was considered an outsider, too, by this person. We were not fit for the ministry—in her eyes. Yet that experience drew us closer to each other and taught us to depend more on God.

I learned early on that there would be times as a family life minister, I would need to buffer my wife and children from those who do not cherish them the way I do. I have been fortunate enough to be married to a wonderful woman who takes most nonsense in stride. Yet I have seen many other spouses deeply hurt by uncaring and critical attitudes by church members. We cannot control what others do, but we can as ministers work to limit their access to and influence on the people we love the most.

These two levels, the personal and the familial, are the foundation for a successful family life ministry. Obviously, when either level is hurting or misunderstood, one's capacity for ministry is compromised. If there are things in my life I need to change, I must as a Christian address these areas. If issues in my marriage or family recur, I must give them the attention they deserve. When unresolved issues are left to fester on these two levels, they will eventually cause significant problems in the family ministry, with the leadership of the church, or within the congregation.

The Programming Level

The change process is often most visible on a programming level. You seek to evaluate and respond to the needs in the church and the community through various programs. (We have discussed this model at length in the chapter on needs analysis.)

How do I stimulate change within the existing programs of the church? Change within existing programs can be accomplished in family ministry only through integration and acceptance. You must learn how the church system is structured and integrate your efforts at appropriate points within the existing structure. You must also work toward congregational acceptance of the programs and timetable. Family ministry is a new philosophy of ministry for most church systems. It is built upon many assumptions that are unfamiliar to ministers and church staffs. To suppose that new assumptions will be adopted immediately is to invite disaster.

Because family ministry is needs analysis based, it brings to the forefront the goals and direction of the entire church. For instance, members who learn 50 percent of the church's adults need counseling must ask some pointed questions: How do we respond to these immediate needs? Do we expand our foreign mission program or address the issues here at home? And if our identity has always been tied to being a mission-minded church, will we see this shift as a defeat or as a victory? Will we view these people in need as wounded sheep looking for the healing Master?

Because of the questions it asks, family ministry generally threatens the status quo. For the most part, as we observed in the earlier chapters, our churches have done a poor job of pastoral care. When a shift in emphasis is called for, it forces the church to ask questions at the deepest level: Why do we exist? What is our mission? How do we measure success in the kingdom right here? It is not surprising that many churches that embrace family ministry often rethink their basic assumptions about ministry.

Because change is a threatening process, you must cultivate relationships with the pulpit minister and other staff men and women who lead the major ministries of the church. Through these ministries, the basic values of the church are given expression. If basic values or assumptions come into question, so do ministry expressions. It is important, therefore, for you to work with the existing ministries.

The change process can often be furthered by implementing family ministry programming through the existing structures of the congregation before building new ones. If that can be accomplished, you and the ministry will be more readily accepted.

I have described family ministry to fellow staff ministers as a filling station. We exist to service the needs of people and leaders in the various ministries as they attempt to meet the needs of family members. We try to develop the philosophy that the church does not have one family life minister; it has many, all working together toward a common vision.

Do I emphasize programming rebirth? We need new models and examples to meet the diverse needs of families. Ministerial models and programs should be reborn almost yearly. New areas of ministry include inner city, rural, dual-career marriages, blended families, and the population of older people. An entire ministry model could be built around any one group.

An openness to learning and a creative spirit are required. I know of no other ministry area that offers as much creative opportunity as does family life ministry. The field is not defined. The picture has not been created. The expectations have not been set. When we speak of pulpit work or a youth minister, a certain picture comes to people's minds. But today when we speak of family life ministry, the screen is blank.

The field is open to men and women who are courageous enough to connect with families and energetic enough not to let their ministries grow stale. Programming rebirth is a lifelong challenge to adapt one's skills and ministry to the changing nature of contemporary family needs.

How do I work with the people involved in my ministry? I have never had a problem with volunteer recruitment in family life ministry. My problem has been keeping up with the offers from talented people who see the needs in families and want to respond to them. Family life ministry motivates wonderfully gifted spiritual people to use their talents in the kingdom.

After trying several organizational methods, including structuring the ministry around a small group of leaders and organizing it with a large committee, I have come to rely on the moving squad concept.

Family ministry draws self-motivated people to be involved in the lives of other families. Most of them are ten-talent people who do not need much direct administration or a lot of meetings. I developed my moving squad concept to meet their unique needs.

Using this model, I look for a person or small group of people interested in a particular aspect of family life ministry. I discuss with them, one-on-one, the nature and function of the ministry to be launched. At times they bring the idea to me. If it is feasible, we begin a mentoring relationship. I challenge them to study, read, and expand their understanding of the ministry, and we build a committed team excited about the same vision. This small group becomes my moving squad.

They are brought together for the express purpose of addressing a ministry need. They are results oriented and focused. They are self-motivated because they will not be in the squad if they do not share the motivating vision. The commitment period is negotiable. For some squads, their time with the family ministry may be extended because the needs are ongoing. For others, they may fulfill their mission and retire from active service. Some, like our Backstage Family Theater group, function at various times of the year. Organization, reports, and administrative meetings are kept to a minimum. We handle those things primarily through the ministry and encourage the people to be involved in direct ministry service.

So you can become a resource manager working with many large and small moving squads—all committed to family life ministry. You can handle meetings and agendas informally over lunches, at breakfasts, or in the office of the squad leader. The ownership of the ministry is broadened to include many members of the church. The creative resource base is deepened because people are creative only about things they are interested in. People are affirmed and valued for their contributions, and you function in one of your most important roles—a trainer of lay ministers.

How does family ministry balance programs with people? Programming has at its essence the meeting of needs. That is why it exists. If the needs do not exist, neither should the program. So programming is people centered. Its heart is in ministry. To suggest that these are separate entities is to misunderstand the nature of both.

In practical terms, you may want to plan on terminating some programs from year to year. Or you may want to offer one year of programs and then start over fresh the next with a clean slate. Although this may not be appropriate for counseling needs, it is certainly a possibility for the preventive side of the ministry. People enjoy novelty and variety. The ability to create new and different approaches will challenge you to stay fresh in your methods.

It is also important to constantly assess the effectiveness of programs. Many churches fall into the event trap. They move from one event to another with little time spent evaluating where they have been or where they are going. Family ministry, because it does surface so many needs, must constantly ask whether the time and effort devoted to a particular family event produce the desired outcome. So programs are created to meet collective needs of people, and people benefit from programs that are tailored to their specifications. Programming is a tool to minister to people.

The Church Leadership Level

Family ministry is often initiated within a local congregation because one leader or a small group of leaders has caught a vision for it. This vision may be the by-product of family stresses in their own lives.

The leaders' understanding of family ministry may be limited. Some may see it as only counseling. Others may view it as a ministry to their particular hobby. Certainly, one or two will be skeptical and will need to be convinced of the need for the ministry.

To be a successful change agent within the existing leadership structure, you must ask several key questions concerning the church, the leadership, and the change process itself.

Do the leaders view this as valid ministry? You will recall that this question was presented as the critical beginning point for the ministry. I believe it is a question that you must visit and revisit with the leaders. You must constantly restate the case for family ministry because the field is so new and the assumptions are often misunderstood.

Family ministry can assist a local church leadership because it addresses the skills that hamstring many leaderships. Family ministry is concerned with interpersonal relations. It sees conflict as a necessary part of the growth process and teaches people how to work through their conflict. It builds group process skills. Leaders are developed internally and given the support to lead a ministry area independently. The interpersonal skills addressed by family ministry can be vital to leaders of the local church.

How do you influence these leaders? I like to provide our leaders with reading materials. I will recommend a chapter of a book and ask them to comment on it. I occasionally write summary papers of materials I think are significant for them. I ask them to attend conferences and set aside money so they and their spouses can attend family ministry events. I involve them in family situations, where appropriate, rather than relieve them totally of the burden of responsibility. Through these ways, they are able to see how family ministry actually functions in the lives of people.

Do I understand the church leadership change range I am working within? Dr. Win Arn reported in his *Growth Report Newsletter* that when a proposal for change was introduced in a church, people would fall into one of five categories. They could be represented by a bell-shaped curve. (See fig. 8.2.)

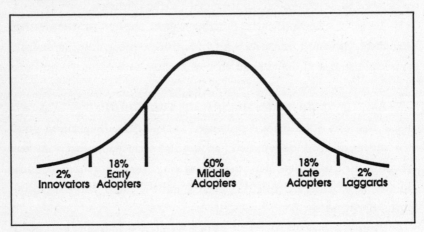

Fig. 8.2. Change range

Innovators. They are the dreamers, persons who are responsible for new ideas but seldom receive credit. They are generally not acknowledged as leaders or policy makers.

Early adopters. They know a good idea when they see it. Their opinions are normally respected in the church, and they often receive credit for a new idea that may not have been theirs.

Middle adopters. The majority respond to the proposals of others. Generally reasonable in their analysis of a new idea, they may prefer to move slower in implementation.

Late adopters. The last in a church to endorse an idea, they often speak against and vote against an idea, change, or innovation. They may never verbally acknowledge acceptance, but they generally adopt it if the majority demonstrate support.

Laggards. New ideas seldom, if ever, are adopted by this group. Their commitment is to the status quo.

Because family life ministry as a movement within the church is in an innovating stage, you need to know how to manage the change process. You must first gauge where the leaders are within this change range. Are they split, with a few innovators dragging laggards along? Are they middle adopters who have hired a staff of innovators and are dragging their feet? Here are some suggestions for working with the local leadership as you implement family life ministry:

- Realize that the capacity to be a change agent within the church system is directly related to the confidence earned by those in the system. If you are perceived as a wise and trustworthy leader, your proposals will be regarded more favorably.
- Realize that once you are inside a church system, your ability to effect changes on certain levels decreases simply by virtue of being a member of the system.
- There is no substitute for positive results. It is difficult to object to something that changes lives and helps families.
- Learn to use the formal and informal communication channels within the church.
- Capitalize on the support of early adopters in the church who can align with the proposed changes and speak to the middle adopters.
- Realize conflict is unavoidable in any church system, and learn to work through it. Distinguish carefully between wars, battles, skirmishes, and warning flares.
- Silence may be the most powerful persuader when it allows time for the results of the ministry to surface.
- Positive ministry can be carved out of the sheer rock of opposition. You, as a minister, have the option of how you will behave in any given situation.
- Accept that there will be alliances and coalitions within the power structure. Strive for a relationship with all groups, aiming

to be seen as an honest broker with the best interests of the church at heart.

- Develop a close relationship with one or two leaders who can be confidants during difficult situations.
- Be mindful of the inherent lack of confidentiality on all levels of the church system.
- Realize it is very difficult to significantly change an existing church system in a short period of time. Some leaders will make significant changes, others will move slightly, while others will make no changes whatsoever. Family ministry can still operate within these parameters.

Businesspeople speak of the "challenge up, support down" rule. In companies I have worked with, it was expected that dissatisfied employees would first challenge up the chain of command. Their responsibility was to support the final decision with subordinates. So the "challenge up, support down" rule was intended to get gripes out on the table with the people who could address them and short-circuit the rumor mill.

The same general principle holds true in family ministry. My responsibility as a minister is to challenge up the line of authority the policies, attitudes, rules, or events that I believe unhealthy for the church family. In this way I am fulfilling my ministry as a spokesperson for the family of faith. At the same time, if I register a complaint or ask for a particular change and am denied, it is my responsibility to support that decision down the line.

No one bats a thousand with proposals. In fact, hindsight will prove for most of us that it was a blessing we were not allowed to implement some changes we believed in so strongly. But the family minister who takes the defeat personally and sows the seeds of discord among ministry leaders or in the congregation is inviting disaster. The minister is cutting the cords of support and trust with the rest of the leaders.

The Congregational Level

We discussed the importance of change within the entire congregation in the chapter on needs analysis. This area of change is most often spoken of when we consider family life ministry. However, if you are not aware of changes on the other four levels of ministry, your work with the congregation will be hampered. All levels must be managed effectively to build stronger Christian families.

Is the ministry producing fire on the fringe? A byproduct of family life ministry is the excitement that it generates among fringe members of the church. These people for one reason or another have been screened out of involvement or active leadership. Their family type may not match the norm of the congregation. Perhaps a single person, a businesswoman, or a divorced person who has ten talents to contribute has never been given the opportunity.

In my experience family ministry produces fire on the fringe of the church. In other words, disenfranchised people who have dreamed of being involved in meaningful ministry discover they are needed. It is not unusual to be approached by people who report they have been members for five, ten, or fifteen years in a congregation and have not been involved. Yet the dreams for family ministry constitute a challenge that they would like to be involved in.

Some of the greatest servants I have worked with in family ministry have been the quiet fringers who have graced the back seats of church auditoriums for decades. They are the hall wanderers and the silent members seated close to the exits. But the validity of family ministry touches a familiar chord in their lives. These people have been wounded by life, but they can become marvelous ministers of healing.

I have already said that family ministry elicits a variety of responses within a local church. Some will move away from the ministry because the truths of family life strike too close to home. Others will move against the ministry because it violates the denial patterns they have cultivated for so many years. But often, the greatest resource to a young family ministry will be the fringers who realize the validity of this work in their own lives and in the community. They are a valuable resource that should not be overlooked.

Is the teaching ministry connecting with people? If a major function of a family life ministry is to provide preventive training and enrichment, effective teaching skills are vital to its success. This is especially true on a congregational level. Outstanding teaching, whether it is small group, preaching, or classroom work, should be your goal.

You are in a unique role to see and evaluate major areas of concern within the corporate church. While it is inappropriate for you to publicly address specific cases, it is appropriate for you to address certain themes within the church.

You may also want to experiment with teaching methodologies. Much of your teaching is deductive in nature. That is, you begin with general principles and assumptions and move to specifics. Adult teaching may get mired in theory and never move to application.

You may want to incorporate an inductive approach to adult teaching. Inductive teaching begins by building a bridge to the learners through cases and specific examples that are directly related to the learners. These specifics are then used to illustrate larger, more complex principles of family life.

We become interested in parenting when we have children. We are sold on good youth ministers when our kids hit the junior high years. A retirement program looks attractive as we approach that stage of development. Inductive learning methods capitalize on knowing where learners are and starting there by building a bridge. They are especially helpful if you are interested in connecting real-life applications to classes and audiences.

Summary

In this chapter we have explored the five levels of change that you must manage. These levels are constantly fluctuating. They include the dynamics within your personality and family, and the complexity of your ministry, leadership, and congregation.

You must work to manage your personal resources. There is only so much spiritual, mental, and emotional gas in the tank to give. Your resources of time and energy must be spent in fruitful ways, given the enormity of family demands in any congregation.

9

COUNSELING, PEOPLE HELPING, AND COUNSELING CENTER MINISTRIES

I was in the middle of a counseling session when my secretary knocked softly on the door interrupting me. "Could you step outside here for just a moment?" she asked, her eyes wide with alarm.

Outside in the reception area was a young woman about thirty years old. She had deep circles under her eyes. Her bulky sweater partially covered several bruises on her arms. She was trying very hard to maintain her composure and not cry.

The story began to tumble out uncontrollably. Her husband had just left town on a business trip. The night before, he had beaten her. It was a pattern, a long and shameful pattern, that she had kept to herself for several years. Now, in his fits of uncontrollable rage, he was threatening her life.

She had no close relatives living in town and very little money. But if she could just get to the home of some friends, she knew they would help her. A phone call was made and a bag was quickly packed. By dinnertime the terrified young woman was taking the first steps in a long journey to putting her life back together.

About five years later, I was speaking at a conference. After my lecture, a woman with a darling little boy came up and introduced herself to me. "You don't remember me, do you?" she asked. I confessed that her eyes were familiar, but I did not.

She said, "I was that terrified young woman you and your secretary helped get to my friends' house several years ago. Your church was like an angel of mercy when I thought there was no hope for my life. And I want to tell you something else. The day I came to you for help I had no idea I was expecting my son. But I know if I had stayed in that abusive situation, I would never have carried the baby to full term. So two scared people came to your office that day, me and another known only by God."

Many churches begin their discussions about family life ministry based on the need for counseling expressed by their members. In this chapter we will look at the role of Christian counseling in the local church. The suggested model presupposes an agreement to a more comprehensive family ministry that is preventive in nature. The ministry of counseling can be greatly enhanced by a proactive developmental family ministry. The two work in a complementary way, one preparing families for crises and the other assisting them through crises.

Pastorless Churches

Before we begin our discussion of Christian counseling, we should consider the critical need for pastoral care in churches. By pastoral care, I am referring to the nurture offered by ministers to their congregations.

During the past two decades, the church growth movement has

made significant and meaningful contributions. As many churches have moved from the country to the city, we have seen the adoption in some quarters of the "bigger is better" philosophy. Some church memberships are touted and sold like memberships to the local health club.

Numerical growth is wonderful, and I am well aware of the significant numbers of conversions recorded in the book of Acts. However, in some quarters church membership is for the healthy and strong. Weak or needy members are seen as liabilities to the more important ministry of expanding the numerical borders of the kingdom. In extreme cases they are encouraged to look elsewhere for a church home, which may be the greatest blessing they ever received.

I believe this subtle movement comes from at least two sources: one philosophical, the other personal. When ministers view their congregations from a success-only standpoint, they are adopting a cultural philosophy and applying it to the church. Success in terms of more members, larger buildings, larger staffs, greater notoriety, and praise becomes an end in itself. A very subtle shift then occurs. Members become mere resources to be used and used up. Members with money, influence, power, and status move quickly to the head of the line in terms of services. People with pain, problems, and pressures are shuffled off to an associate minister who is semiretired and has time for the pastoral care of the church. The minister has adopted a success ethic of ministry that views personal and family problems as inconvenient exit ramps off the main highway of mission. The unspoken rule becomes, "Go take care of your problems and then come back and see us."

A second source of this shift has to do with the personal makeup of the minister. I believe the ranks of ministry are filled with men and women who have never explored the complexities of their personalities, motivations, and histories. They know little about themselves. They unknowingly bring these biases and motivations into ministry, anoint them at the altar, and inflict them on an unsuspecting church. How frequently has a preacher's anger sounded like the railings of a rejected child? How often has a ministry family moved because the minister does not know how to walk through conflict? The need for ministers to face themselves is critical. And as more and more people enter ministry from business and industry, exploring this process further will be imperative.

Pastorless churches develop class systems. Members who are useful in terms of feeding the success ethic of the church move to the forefront of attention. Members who are less personally or financially fortunate are left to their own devices and expected to cheer on the more fortunate few. The blessed are not challenged to meaningful commitments, the hurting in the pew suffer in silence before leaving, and ministers do not grow in their ability to minister to people.

The most critical need in our churches is the need for basic pastoral care. Congregations are dying for ministers who will walk with them through the trials and complexities of life. Ministers must cease to be performers under bright lights and become costrugglers under transparent lights. We need a generation of ministers who feel the calling of God to serve a congregation of people through the life span.

Pastoral care is not an add-on ministry to the work of the local church. It cannot be a third-string job description for a retiring minister coming home off the mission field. It must be a dynamic part of the work of each minister.

The purpose of the church is to show the character of God in all areas of life. We show that character through our worship, edification, and evangelism. But all three missions suffer when we neglect or abandon the basic care of the saints. This care is ongoing, long-term, and dynamically interrelated. In the span of one week, our staff worked with a man who had an incurable illness, a family that had lost a child at birth, a woman who learned her husband was having an affair, a member who fired another member from his business, the family of a longtime member who died after an extended illness, two men who lost their jobs in a bank buyout, and a teen who was hospitalized following a car accident.

These are not extraordinary cases. This is the fabric of contemporary ministry in the local church. Each person suffers in a unique way. Each person experiences short-term and long-term consequences of the trauma. Every person asks vital spiritual questions that need wise counsel.

Pastoral care is only one level of response available to the local church. A family ministry can help a church develop multiple levels of response to the various emotional, psychological, and spiritual needs of members. I call it the funnel model.

Levels of Counseling Response: The Funnel Model

Some ministers describe their frustration after spending an enormous amount of time and energy on a counseling case only to find that person reverts to past patterns of behavior or the behavior is so unpredictable as to defy explanation. Church leaders should have a clear picture of the nature and severity of the counseling needs they are facing when they visit with people.

At the top of the funnel model is a wide opening, representing a large available pool of people and a fairly ordinary issue or problem. As we descend into the funnel, the issues become more acute, the response becomes more sophisticated, and the available pool of people to help becomes more limited. By understanding where an issue falls in a general way, a family minister can help the church gauge what an appropriate response would be. (See fig. 9.1.)

Let's now examine each level of response. Levels 1 through 3 can be provided by any church given the appropriate training. Level 4 can be added through a family life ministry.

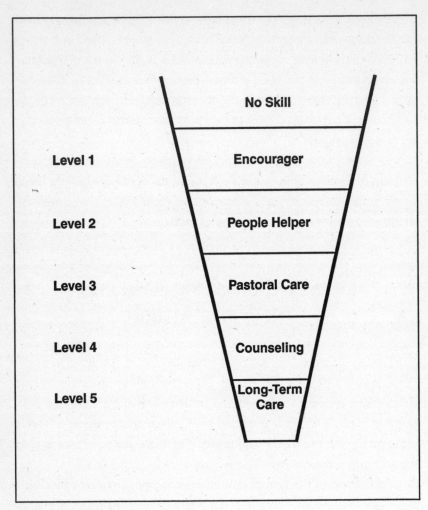

	No Skill
Level 1	**Encourager**
Level 2	**People Helper**
Level 3	**Pastoral Care**
Level 4	**Counseling**
Level 5	**Long-Term Care**

Fig. 9.1. The funnel model

No Skill and No Help!

Many people in the church have no people skills whatsoever. Everyone they come into contact with needs some patching up when they walk away. They are basically unskilled, unnoticing, and unknowing. They will likely never drop in to the work of people helping because it seems messy.

Although they may be of no direct help, they may be a great asset as supporters of the work. Many will say how glad they are family ministry is present so someone else can deal with the problems of all the hurting people. Others will take a passive role as spectators of the enormous problems in the church.

Encouragers

Acts 4 speaks of Barnabas as a "Son of Encouragement" (v. 36). All church members should be trained as responsible encouragers to the rest of the body of Jesus Christ. They should be taught the skills of helpfulness. They should master active listening skills. They should be articulate and be able to cultivate natural people skills. I am amazed at how often the New Testament writers encouraged the early church to be courteous and Christian in their communications. With these skills firmly implanted in the response mechanism of the church, members will begin to be more open to the struggles and problems we all face.

The pulpit minister can take the lead in fostering the congregation as encouragers. Helping them see the overall value of each member being kind, understanding, and compassionate to one another will build the sense of family within the church. You are not trying to make everyone in the pew a junior counselor. You are trying to build healthy Christian interpersonal relations that will go a long way to building a functional church family.

Let me add one other concept to the model—zone of impact. Zone of impact refers to the numbers of people that a person may touch with helping skills. From a helping standpoint, unskilled people will have little or no effective zone of impact. The zone of impact for encouragers will be limited but important to the life of the church. They may be Bible class teachers, zone leaders, or women's group coordinators. They may not come into contact with as many people on an intimate level as a family life minister, but they may be the first people to sense a problem is present. Or in many cases they may be the first persons others in crises confide in. If the persons are trained in basic encouraging skills and know how to recognize the signs of a serious problem, they can encourage the hurting individuals to seek additional help.

People Helpers

Some Christians have the gift of listening and discernment. They are wise, often beyond their years. They have deep compassion for people in difficulty, but they are able to set appropriate boundaries and not become rescuers. They have many times been through traumas themselves and have come to a deeper understanding of life, God, and Jesus Christ. These people can be groomed and trained as people helpers in the local church.

I will say more about the training of these servants in the church later in this chapter, but a few words of introduction are needed at this juncture. They are first and foremost compassionate listeners. They will require ongoing training and direct supervision by the family life minister. Their zone of impact will be limited. They will work within their natural networks of small groups, ministries, and Bible classes. They can help people clarify their concerns and assist them to professional help if that is required. They can also augment the work of the counseling staff. One couple I worked with who had coped with the death of a teenage son became excellent people helpers and often joined me in a counseling session to relate their story and how they dealt with their grief. Their testimony was much more powerful than anything I could deliver.

People helpers can be assets to the family ministry, but care should be taken in their selection and training and the zone of impact they are allowed to function within.

Staff Pastoral Care

As I stated earlier, the need is great for ongoing pastoral care as a basic part of the tool kit for every church. Some ministers will have more formalized training. All ministers can and should participate in continuing education to familiarize themselves with the changing nature of contemporary family problems.

Church leaders should view retooling as an investment in the minister, the members who benefit from the minister's training, and the overall effectiveness of the program of the church. This retooling should also include clear discussions of the limits of each minister's expertise. I generally find ministers counseling far beyond the limits of their abilities, which creates an unhealthy situation for everyone.

However, I am also pleased to see the positive results that can be achieved by a caring, pastoral minister who has received training and is using personal gifts. Ken Snell, an associate minister on our staff, regularly offers a grief recovery support group. He has trained specifically in that area of ministry and repeatedly does an excellent job in building a sense of caring Christian community within the groups he leads. His sense of timing and use of story and metaphor leave many on my clinical staff watching in amazement. One woman stated after the group was finished, "I never really felt like I belonged in this church until this group came along. Now I feel like there are people here who are just like me."

The zone of impact for pastorally gifted ministers can be moderate to large. In fact, they may have to set some limits on the time they spend in pastoral care given the family needs in every church. The benefits far outweigh the negatives. Churches are starving for ministers who remember the sheep instead of driving as fast as they can for the next pasture. The regular walk with men and women through the valley of the shadow of death is the basis of vital ministry.

Christian Counseling

The growing need for individual, marital, and family counseling within the local church is occurring at an alarming rate. Congregations are facing more and more cases that require longer term care and professional intervention.

When I first began conducting needs analysis with congregations considering family life ministry, we would ask whether each adult member knew of a need for individual, marital, or family counseling in his or her family. It was fairly common for one-third of the congregation to answer affirmatively. In my more recent studies ten years later, the numbers may easily go as high as 50 percent. Unquestionably, Christian counseling will play a larger role in the ministry of the church and, I believe, will soon be seen as an expectation among larger, multiple staff congregations.

Some congregations approach the need for Christian counseling through building a referral network with local counselors or members in private practice. This approach can serve a congregation well provided there is a clear understanding of expectations on the part of the church leaders and the practitioners. Misunderstandings can arise when payments, fee schedules, and limits of confidentiality are not clearly understood.

A congregation may opt to bring in a Christian counselor on a limited basis, working a specified day each week. This arrangement may allow the counselor to maintain a private practice in another location and still offer a valuable ministry to the church.

Churches that choose to begin a full-time counseling ministry will need to consider a myriad of detail questions. We will address some later in this chapter. Although a full-time therapist may meet the therapeutic needs of the church, expecting that individual to automatically implement and execute a family life ministry is another matter entirely. If those expectations exist, they should be clearly defined, and the counselor should be informed at the outset.

The person may lack both the knowledge and the expertise to develop a family life ministry.

Not every congregation can afford a full- or part-time staff person in the area of family life ministry or Christian counseling, but church cooperation could be a win-win situation for everyone involved. Churches in outlying regions could contract with a counselor to travel circuit-rider fashion from town to town, working with a different church each day of the week. Preventive programs could be offered and shared among participating congregations. A supervising committee could be established, composed of representatives from each church. Creativity and the willingness to experiment with new models could add dynamic life to churches with limited resources and offer a great ministry to communities struggling with family problems.

Long-Term Care

The need for more intensive long-term psychotherapy and hospitalization is also a growing reality for the family life ministry. Church members and community neighbors are struggling with a whole range of significant problems that are beyond the scope of the local church's response.

Fortunately, many programs of inpatient psychotherapy recognize the need for ongoing spiritual guidance and counsel. They recognize the need for a holistic approach to emotional healing, which includes addressing the spiritual needs of people.

You must act as a wise shepherd discerning what kind of response a particular crisis demands. You must manage cases carefully with an eye toward confidentiality. You must assist the staff in retooling and continually act as a change agent to upgrade the congregation's skills as a caring community of God's people. The funnel model is just one way to conceptualize the nature and extent of the issues being addressed.

What If No One Is There to Help?

As I was completing my graduate work, a wealthy rancher called me concerning his church and community. There were many serious family problems in his town but no one to help. His family had been affected by divorce and addiction, and he wanted to do something about it. His proposal was to bring together a coalition of concerned Christian businesspeople who would underwrite the cost of flying in a therapist once a week to work with clients and conduct groups. The businesspeople would provide free office space and administrative overhead, and the counselor would be paid through the fees collected. Area churches could take advantage of the services, also.

I was impressed with his creativity and get-it-done attitude. There are usually a number of possibilities available to any church interested in providing professional counseling from a Christian perspective. Here are a few options.

1. Bring someone in. As my rancher friend illustrates, there are ways to bring in helpers on a regular but limited basis. Perhaps a counselor in a neighboring area would be willing to work one day a week at the church. A college or university in the area may have professors on staff who would be willing to assist.

2. Retrain existing staff. I have mentioned this several times as a legitimate option. Present staff members may be willing to move into this area of ministry following a period of retraining.

3. Use an internist. Graduate programs in marriage and family therapy require a period of supervised practicum for students. Increasingly, graduate programs are seeing the wisdom in placing these students in environments where they can receive experience away from the university setting. Many graduate programs have men and women who are anxious to use their skills in a local church setting. Consider contacting the directors of these programs for their

specific program policies. An outstanding graduate student may develop into a gifted staff minister for the congregation.

4. Collaborate with another congregation. If churches can learn to collaborate and work together, they may be able to provide services to their members never dreamed of before. Family issues cross all lines. When we come together to discuss concerns, we often discover that we are struggling with very similar sets of circumstances.

5. Check with private practitioners. Men and women in private practice may be open to offering their services to the church. Expectations in terms of confidentiality, fees, and referral processes should be articulated openly. Counselors in private practice are often an excellent source of ideas in building a counseling ministry in the local church. They may know people and programs in the area that the minister can contact.

People Helping

People helping can be one of the most effective and fruitful works of a family life ministry. It can open doors to hidden pain and suffering that would otherwise go unnoticed. It can use a segment of gifts in the church that often go undeveloped.

People helping must also be one of the most closely managed ministries in the family life ministry. It is often the ministry I am asked to initiate with a church and usually one of the last I bring on-line. The reason is simple. We must select, train, and supervise people helpers with the utmost rigor and care.

There are two reasons for the cautious approach. First, the initiation of a family life ministry often surfaces a group of emotionally unstable people who are looking for an opportunity to overinvolve themselves in the lives of others. They may have a need to be rescuers. They may delight in knowing and spreading information about others. They may be working out their own problems through unhealthy helping relationships with others. Whatever the motivation, they will often be the first in line declaring, "Dr. Don, you cannot believe all the people who tell me their problems." Normally, that is a red flag.

The second reason deals with the nature of therapy itself. People helpers are not junior counselors. They are not psychologists. They are empathetic listeners who try to provide compassion and understanding as other people work through their issues. Many people enter people helper training with an expectation that they are going to learn how to help fix people's problems. Nothing could be further from the truth. Individuals looking for a ministry credential to anoint their homegrown problem-solving philosophy can do more damage in one week than a family minister can clean up in a month.

So, what kinds of people make good people helpers? Some characteristics include

- the ability to listen and understand experiences outside a personal range of experience.
- a nonjudgmental spirit.
- an openness to learning.
- the ability to articulate the concepts of biblical grace, forgiveness, community of faith, prayer, and intercession; the work of the Spirit; and the active love of God through Jesus Christ.
- a spirit of compassion in the face of human suffering.
- a deep love for people seen through a broad range of associations.
- patience with change and with other people's ability to gain insight.
- the ability to maintain healthy boundaries and not be responsible for others as rescuers.
- self-awareness. These people understand their personalities and temperaments. They are aware of the baggage they carry and its impact on their Christian worldview.

• a deep and abiding scar. The best people helpers can identify with pain because they have felt pain and walked through it rather than denied its existence.

Integrating Counseling and Family Ministry

I have said that preventive and therapeutic efforts in a family life ministry feed off each other and bless each other's efforts. As counseling explores themes and patterns of unhealthy families, we identify areas of proactive training. As training is offered, those in counseling receive additional skills to manage their problems more effectively.

The local church is in an ideal role to offer integrated training and therapy because both ministries reflect the basic nature of the church itself. As preventive programs are planned and as therapeutic responses are considered, they should be designed to complement each other.

For example, a person calling the family life minister for help could be referred to one of several resources or a combination of resources to help her address her needs. Such a multilevel response might include counseling with a Christian counselor, attending a support group, reading a book or listening to a tape, attending a class, seminar, or retreat, or receiving assistance from an appropriate referral source. All of these responses could be designed, given the development of a comprehensive family ministry program (see fig. 9.2).

Using this model, you, the family life minister, can call on the various levels of responses offered by the local church. Each level of response can operate within its area of competency and expertise. You are called not to deliver therapy but to address areas of specific spiritual concern. Counseling loads can be eased as people work in groups or are listened to by trained compassionate listeners.

You must play two key roles in this model. First, you must manage the various cases and be aware of the ways in which the ministry

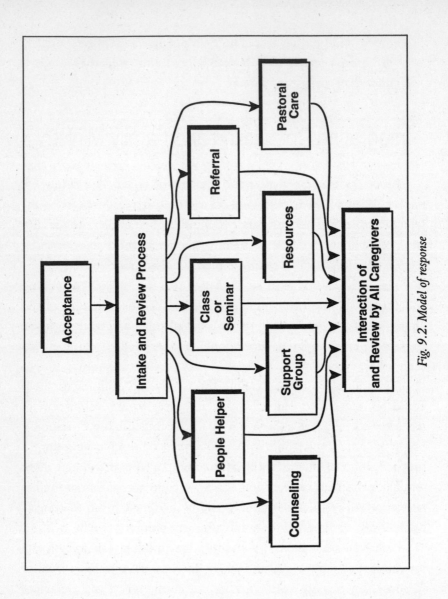

Fig. 9.2. Model of response

is responding to various cases and crises. You must take care that the various elements working with an individual do not work at cross purposes. Also, you must respect and guard the primary confidentiality of all clients working with the counseling ministry.

The second key role you must play is that of trainer and equipper. Skilled people helpers must be trained, equipped, and supervised. Resources must be reviewed, produced, edited, and distributed. Support groups must be organized and supervised. Referral networks must be set up. The task of organizing and administering the therapeutic response is enormous and can quickly become the primary time-consuming task of ministry. The good news is, once these systems are in place and operational, they increase your ability to respond to the need for counseling and pastoral care.

People Helpers Planted in Networks

Pastorless churches may be characterized by a lack of care within the networks of the body. All churches have formal and informal networks: the nursery workers, the women's choral group, the Saturday morning men's breakfast gang, or one of many small groups in the church. These groups form the network around which the church is built.

These groups serve many useful purposes. They allow communications to permeate throughout the congregation. Positive information can be planted within them and passed from network to network. They are the birthplace of opinions and congregational attitude. They are the genesis of dreams and the discussion groups that accept or reject the dreams. Church consultants have known for years the importance of tapping into the mood and tenor of the congregational networks to measure congregational health.

These networks are also the first line of defense in people helping. When family problems arise, small groups notice them first. Someone is upset. A couple that was once highly involved now takes a back seat. A loss occurs, and the church fails to respond appropriately.

When networks fail to have trained people helpers (incidentally, I believe this is a modern idea for the New Testament concept of shepherds), they are at risk. Problems can develop, or people may go through a crisis without one person there to offer Christian support and concern. Disappointment and disillusionment occur, and members eventually begin to fall through the cracks.

When networks have trained people helpers, they can be alert to people problems. They can be there to listen and express concern. They can check out subtle messages of pain or worry. They can clue ministers and church leaders to the need for professional help or pastoral care.

Some churches have many networks. Some are overlapping and have contact with other networks. Others rarely interact with each other. Without an internal shepherding function they lack a vital ingredient for building congregational health.

Now imagine some trained people helpers ministering to the same congregation's networks. Scattered informally throughout the congregation, they can assist in pastoral care. I am not suggesting a formalized program where certain people are assigned to certain groups. The wise family life minister is able to discern the networks that exist and determine if someone in each one could be trained as a people helper.

Certainly, not all networks will have trainable people, and some groups may need more assistance than others. But the results of planting servant-hearted listeners in the church can be amazing. I recall working with a team of twenty people helpers. One couple in the church was experiencing severe marital difficulties and was receiving counsel outside the church. When the news came that the marriage was ending in divorce, I received four phone calls in one morning from people helpers. Two of them had befriended the wife and had been ministering to her; two had befriended the husband and stood close to him. None had been involved in advice giving or undermining the therapeutic process, and none of them knew of the activities of the others! They had independently seen a need and responded with complete confidentiality without overstepping the definition of their roles. Though the marriage eventually ended, the concept of people helping was demonstrated.

Approaches to Training

Churches vary in their levels of training of people helpers. Some use planned curricula designed to equip members with the skills to do active listening and basic problem solving. Others rely on one-shot weekend seminars with visiting content experts training lay leaders.

A comprehensive program of people helping should include training encouragers, selecting and screening potential people helpers, initial training, self-assessment exercises, ongoing supervision, and follow-up intensive training. Let's explore each phase and the goals to be accomplished.

Training Encouragers

The goal of this phase is to increase the congregation's awareness of and participation in encouraging interpersonal relations skills. The goal is to create a more caring Christian community within the local church. Methods can include sermons, classes, videos, and weekend seminars.

Selecting and Screening Potential People Helpers

After you have become acquainted with the church, you may want to invite a short list of potential people helpers for an initial conversation about the ministry. If you do not know the congregation well, you may want to ask other staff ministers or leaders for potential candidates. Include a description of the role and function of the person to be selected. I use a brief questionnaire to get some idea of the person's background and training in helping. Those who seem to possess the necessary gifts and heart for this ministry are invited to participate in an orientation meeting.

Initial Training

The first level of training will acquaint the beginning people helper with basic helping skills. In our church, we set the context of people helping in its biblical framework. We show how people helping fits in with the work of the local church and the family ministry specifically. We discuss the characteristics of an effective people helper and offer a beginning model of helping.

People helper training can, and I believe should, be approached with a level of expectation that exceeds the normal Sunday school class. We have strict attendance expectations. We require the purchase of books and assign homework each week. We test throughout the class. We are not trying to create graduate students, but we want people to gain an effective mastery of the concepts. We aim the training, approximately, at a college freshman or sophomore level as closely as we can.

Often, the initial training period weeds out those who are not serious about the ministry or may feel their gifts do not match the expectations after all. We openly encourage people to assess their competency as they progress through the course.

Self-Assessment Exercises

Each level of training includes some activity to help individuals gain a greater understanding of their personality makeup, family history, temperament, and events that went into shaping their identity. This is a critical factor in building and maintaining a core of healthy people helpers.

People helpers must be carefully and tenderly trained in the process of looking constantly in the mirror. We use several tools to help people understand themselves better before they try to understand others.

Typically, many potential people helpers approach this phase of training with apprehension. Confidentiality must be maintained, and the process should be explained in a positive way. Experience has shown that this phase of training almost always receives the highest marks from students.

Results of this phase are often communicated one-on-one with the family life minister. At this time the minister can discuss the impact of the first level of training and the desirability to continue with additional training.

Ongoing Supervision

The initiation of a people helping ministry necessitates ongoing supervision from you. Set aside time to meet regularly with people helpers and continue their training one-on-one or in groups. This can also be a time to integrate other staff ministers who are counseling with members into a supervision session.

It is both unwise and unethical to train people helpers and then turn them loose in a congregation without any supervision or ministerial guidance. To do that is to invite the junior counselor syndrome. People helpers must be reminded they are not therapists; they are to listen and refer to others when the situation warrants.

Follow-Up Intensive Training

Once an initial group of people helpers has been trained, you will want to continue the training in both general and specific areas of ministry.

In our church, we refer to our helpers on three levels: helpers, people helpers, and skilled helpers. Those who have been through an initial level of training are helpers. People helpers receive additional training in human development, adult development, helping models, and other topics to create a deeper understanding of the helping process. Skilled helpers are rare individuals with a combination of gifts, training, and life experiences to address a particular life crisis or concern. A young mother who lost twins may eventually train to help other mothers work through their grief. A widow may help other widows through the legal, emotional, and financial adjustments after the loss of the spouse. An ex-drug offender may lead a support group. Whatever the area of involvement, these servants possess all the necessary ingredients to speak authentically to a specific life crisis.

As I have already mentioned, each stage of training includes some self-assessment activity. The longer the person works as a people helper, the more personal the training becomes. Eventually, it grows into self-study with the family minister functioning as a resource person and mentor.

Counseling Centers and the Church

Some churches will choose to expand the family life ministry with the initiation of a counseling office or counseling center. This subject justifies treatment by an entire book, but I would like to address some of the most common questions asked by church leaders as they consider launching a counseling center.

How do we begin addressing the need for a counseling center?

I suggest a feasibility study of the church, the available resources, and the surrounding community. The study might be conducted by an outside consultant who has directed a center and can bring questions to the table that might otherwise be overlooked. The feasibility study should address the nature of the community, the kinds of services needed, the services offered by other churches and agencies, and budget and facility recommendations. The family ministry committee could work to develop the study and overall plan of action.

If we choose to go ahead, what plan must be developed to launch a center?

A great deal of preliminary work should go into the operations and administration of a counseling center. Operational plans should address the following areas:

- A business plan
- Philosophy and goals for the center, including an agreed-upon theory of change
- An operations manual defining administrative and clinical practices for the staff
- Definition of fees, schedules, collections, and accounting procedures
- Insurance coverage for clinical staff, board of directors, and property
- Legal considerations, decisions on incorporation and licensure in the state
- Referral sources and networking opportunities
- Staffing requirements and procedures
- Record keeping and secretarial procedures
- Issues of supervision of staff, confidentiality, and professional development
- Scholarship procedures for needy cases
- Relationship with staff and church leadership defined
- Role of support and therapy groups
- Advertising and marketing services

These issues should be discussed within the ministry and with the church leadership as a whole. Everyone needs to start with similar expectations.

What kind of facility should we provide?

I have counseled in renovated farmhouses, church offices, and converted classrooms bordering noisy gymnasiums. So long as strict privacy can be provided and the atmosphere can set the client at ease, many settings can serve the needs.

Many churches have opted to purchase homes adjacent or near to the church building to provide a location for their counseling staff. Renovated homes are wonderful because they tend to provide needed flexibility. They also present a less formal atmosphere.

Can we use the church offices?

Church offices normally do not provide the necessary confidentiality or atmosphere conducive to the therapeutic process. Members are concerned about staff and secretaries knowing who is coming for an appointment. The church is sent the wrong message about the importance of the need for privacy. Setting up an auxiliary office somewhere away from the main church office but within the church building is preferable to using the main area.

Should we charge for counseling?

I have spoken with many directors of Christian counseling centers through the years concerning the issue of charging for therapy. Almost without exception they recommend that clients pay something for therapy. Having counseled in settings with no charge, sliding scales, and flat fees, I tend to agree.

The directors cited the following reasons for charging for therapy:

- It actively involves the client in the process.
- Whether they admit it or not, people tend to value things they pay something for.
- Counseling services are viewed by many church leaders and members as beyond the scope of normal ministerial services provided by the local church.
- Experience indicates that people who pay little or nothing tend to be the most demanding administratively, the least motivated to change, the most critical, and the most likely to drop out of the therapeutic process.

What about sliding scales?

Sliding scales can be beneficial to people who need therapy but are limited due to financial constraints. A sliding scale is normally tied to gross family income and sets an hourly fee based on a predetermined range.

One common flaw in sliding scales is the tendency for everyone to slide to the bottom of the fee scale. Planning would suggest that clients would fall along a range, but my experience has been that a large segment will underreport their income. The director does not want to be placed in a position of being a financial detective.

A second flaw with sliding scales is designing one fee schedule for church members and another for community people. While in theory this sounds like a fair benefit for church members, the staff and director soon find themselves trying to define who is really a member. Clients will promise to place membership next Sunday when they hear they can get a better deal on the fees! Community people will learn that there is a double standard, and they may be offended by it.

What about flat rate fees?

A center should do a market analysis of the typical rate for Christian and private counseling and then set a flat, fair rate that reflects the ministry objectives of the center and the church. These fees may be charged to members and nonmembers. Clients can be informed that rates have been set below market rate and the fees provide overhead for the center's operation and support for the therapists. Most people readily accept the arrangement and are pleased to find a resource that is more affordable than a community agency or private practitioner.

But what about people who cannot pay?

A good solution is a scholarship fund set up as a part of the church's support for the center. Church leaders can yearly earmark funds, which are then allocated on a monthly basis and assigned to clients based on need.

The current operation of our scholarship fund calls for the family to fill out a brief application. The director reviews it and, after approving it, signs a contract for a specific amount of scholarship support and a specific number of sessions. The client and the therapist also sign at the beginning of therapy. If the client is assigned to a support or therapy group, the therapist forwards a referral form to the group leader.

Once the contracted period has ended, the director and the therapist meet to discuss a continuation or dismissal of the scholarship arrangement. Clients are encouraged to take over the responsibility for payment of their sessions when possible. A general rule of "everyone pays something" seems to be a fair approach and is well received by staff and clients.

How can we involve the church staff with the counseling center staff?

First, both groups must work in concert and see themselves working toward the same ends. Both are concerned with healing broken lives. Second, the counseling staff can provide in-service training and consultation to the ministerial staff. In return the ministry staff can offer feedback concerning the struggles they see within the congregation. Third, the director may want to provide a more formal process whereby a staff member can make a referral to the center providing the information needed to conduct an initial assessment.

Summary

A car stopped in the alley behind the minister's home. He was out washing his car, preparing to move his family out of town the very next day. A woman rolled down her window and called his name.

"So, you're really leaving us, are you?" she smiled. "I don't know who we are going to call up at church now. Everyone is so busy doing things, there doesn't seem to be any time for people like us. It's a shame. It's a real shame that the church my husband and I have devoted over twenty-five years to does not have one minister we would call if there was a problem in our family. Well, you kids take care." With that she drove away.

Churches are dying for a lack of genuine relationships. People want to rediscover their relationships with their spouses and their children. Many are hungry for a meaningful relationship with God. They come and they go, never filling that growing emptiness inside. Too often they fade away, and no one seems to understand why.

Not everyone will need professional counseling. The majority of people may never need a therapy group. But we all need what the woman in that alley was missing in her life—a group of people who genuinely care and a group of ministers who are called to help families. There's a name for that. We call it the church.

10

PREPARATION AND COMPETENCIES OF THE FAMILY LIFE MINISTER

My phone rang on Monday morning before the staff meeting. It was a long-distance call from a minister several states away. He asked if I could visit a few minutes with him about family ministry.

"I met with the leadership of the church last night, and we have decided to expand my ministry to include a ministry to families," he said. "Could we arrange a time for me and some of my key leaders to come over and talk with you about family ministry and setting up a counseling center?"

A few weeks later the delegation arrived. They were full of wonderful ideas and noble intentions. I asked the youth minister who was considering a job shift about his background and preparation for the task. He had not had any formal training in counseling—although he seemed to have the necessary ingredients to be a people helper. He had done some work in preparing preventive programs for the church but only as an adjunct to his youth work. His training in ministry was limited due to his entrance into youth work from a successful career in sales and marketing. The pulpit minister had seen his natural giftedness and encouraged him to pursue youth ministry.

I applauded their good intentions and gently raised a few questions of competencies. How could the church expect this youth minister to respond to the needs of church families with only limited tools in his tool kit? They had never thought of that before.

After some preliminary discussions, they thanked me for my time and returned home. Several weeks later I received a call from the young man. He and his church had struck a creative agreement that would provide him the tools he needed to pursue family ministry and offer the church family care. The church agreed to finance his continued education as a part of a retooling package on a part-time basis. In return for the investment, the youth minister agreed to work an additional period of years as direct repayment.

It was a win-win deal for both sides. The church would receive competent help, and the minister would receive the tools to adequately care for families.

Preparing men and women for the complex job of a ministry to families requires immediate attention. Dennis Guernsey, in his excellent book *A New Design for Family Ministry,* points out the need for a revolution in our thinking concerning family ministers:

Although the large churches are beginning to see the need for this emphasis, the jobs are often filled by those who are not trained for the task. Their motivations are high, and their dedication unquestioned. But the task is too critical to be assigned to someone who has not garnered the skills needed to do an effective job. Bluntly said, without retraining, we cannot afford to give the task to youth pastors who are no longer young or returned missionaries who cannot for some reason continue on in the mission field.

The challenge is clear. We need a new breed of minister trained with special emphasis in the preventive and therapeutic needs of the local church. These new family life ministers should be able to handle much of the counseling and program development of the family life ministry within the congregation.

In this chapter we will explore the major areas of training and the specific competencies necessary to function effectively in the church as a family life minister. We will also look at the issues involved in retooling ministers for careers in family life ministry. Finally, we will explore the hazards of the first year.

An individual must enter family ministry with caution and prayer. The expectations are unique, unlike those of the pulpit, youth, or educational minister. Proper training is the only safeguard for the church's and the minister's well-being.

Areas of Training

Family ministry combines the knowledge and skill base of three vital areas of study: theology, marriage and family counseling, and adult education. (See fig. 10.1.) Let's consider each one briefly.

First, as the family minister, you must be thoroughly trained in theology, ministry, and evangelism. There is no substitute for a knowledge of God's Word as it applies to the family. Ministry skills are absolutely essential for the competent performance of your job on a day-to-day basis.

You should be trained in exegetical skills. You must be knowledgeable in church growth, pastoral care, preaching, teaching, and visitation. You must be able to work confidently with a large staff or alone in a small church setting.

You are first and foremost a minister. You are not a marriage and family therapist who has chosen to pursue your profession within the confines of the local church. I have seen many whose hearts were

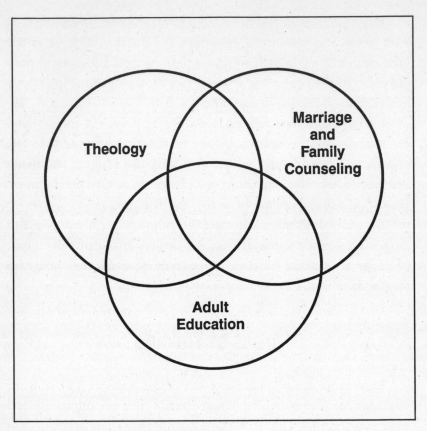

Fig. 10.1. Areas of training for family ministry

devoted to marriage and family therapy enter local church work. They were often frustrated, unfulfilled, and ineffective in building a solid family life ministry. I believe the failures stemmed from a lack of basic training in ministerial skills.

I have been surprised to learn how credibility is built for this role. As a family life minister, when I speak about the family from a strictly psychological or sociological perspective, interest and a degree of respect are generated. But when I can help people see how God's Word and sound psychological principles combine to help people, a new appreciation for God and the ministry becomes evident.

I cannot overstate the need for extensive formal training in ministry as the beginning point for the family life minister. If you come to family ministry from another helping profession, I believe a remedial plan of study should be designed for you that is rigorous and challenging in terms of theological studies. Without that basis you will be at a disadvantage.

Second, you must be a trained marriage and family therapist. Guernsey stated it succinctly, "The new breed of family ministers should be able to handle 80 percent of the counseling problems that walk in the front door of the church and to know when and where to refer the others. They ought not be rookies."

You should be familiar with family systems and how those dynamics affect the local church. You should have gone through rigorous training and dealt with the issues in your family of origin. You should have received quality supervision and be familiar with a wide range of family problems.

Many church leaders I talk with want to appoint someone on staff as a family life minister because the person is available, interested, or empathetic. Church leaders must understand that naming a staff minister as family life minister changes the perception of the congregation. A person may say, "I'm a family life minister, but I tell people that I don't counsel." That does not in any way alter the way the church and the community view the person, however. A family life minister will be viewed as a counselor and will be called on to function in that role.

Many quality programs offer training in marriage and family therapy. You should be encouraged to pursue educational opportunities leading to membership in the American Association for Marriage and Family Therapy and licensure in your state. These credentials add skills, not frills. They are an investment in you and in the church.

Third, you should be familiar with a wide range of practices that are a part of the growing adult education field. Because family ministry is primarily preventive, adult education offers you an opportunity to explore how adults learn and to design and develop programs.

Areas of specialization such as human resource development or training and development provide exposure to theories and practices that are directly applicable to the day-to-day functioning of the ministry. These skills will greatly enhance your effectiveness.

A formal graduate degree may not be required in each area, but a complete program of study should address all three areas. With these skills firmly in place, you will enter the local church with the tools in your tool kit to immediately affect the church in a positive way.

Areas of Competency

I worked for a university that specialized in training returning adults from business settings. The president of that university demanded that the catalog list the competencies of each course. Every instructor and every course were graded by students in light of these competencies.

Job descriptions are often broad and loaded with individual agendas. I prefer to talk in terms of competencies. What competencies must you possess to function effectively as the family life minister in the local church?

Design, Development, and Delivery of Family Life Programs

Coming directly from the field of adult education, you must be able to quickly and efficiently bring on-line a variety of family life ministry offerings. These programs may be large or small, elaborate or simple. You or a trained volunteer may deliver them. Your ability to function creatively will be one of the most important competencies you can master.

Needs Analysis

You must be able to identify the felt needs of the church and the community. You must be able to prioritize these needs and apply resources to meeting these needs. Some skills in statistics and computer science may be helpful. You must be able to translate this data into meaningful reports that move members into action.

Effective Teaching and Preaching

You are primarily a communicator. Whether you are working with a family in distress, a group of people helpers, or the church staff, teaching a class, or preaching on Sunday, your skills in oral communication must be excellent. You win confidence and credibility when you can stand before the congregation and lead them into a study of God's Word as it relates to marriage, parenting, ministry to low-income people, and many other critical themes.

Marriage and Family Therapy

We have already discussed the importance of counseling in any family life ministry. You must be involved in the lives of the people through individual, marital, and family counseling. Group work should be a part of your regular activities.

One word of caution should be noted. It is often a wise idea to design the job description with a certain percentage of your time devoted to counseling and counseling-related activities. The task of counseling is usually enormous and can quickly consume all your time. Soon the church has a staff Christian counselor, which is wonderful, but it is not family life ministry. It is very realistic, at the outset, to discuss backup resources for you when you have reached your maximum number of counseling cases. This is likely to occur within the first year.

Assessing Community Resources and Referrals

The family ministry will depend on a variety of community resources to meet the needs of the family. No church can come close to providing all the necessary services to families. For this reason, you must spend time networking in the community and building a relationship with other counselors, lawyers, hospitals, support groups, and dozens of other professional service providers. No other staff member has the potential for breaking down the barriers between the church and the community like the family life minister.

Program Promotion and Advertising

The best advertising for family life ministry comes through the word of mouth contacts made by church members. Family ministry gives church members a common denominator between themselves and the people they work with or friends in the PTA. It can become the conduit for a family to reestablish ties with estranged parents or children.

One man attended a family life conference on healing broken relationships. After listening to the sessions, he committed himself to restoring his relationship with his estranged father, even though they had not spoken in more than ten years. The next weekend he drove halfway across the state to take the first step in reaching his father. Today they visit regularly and have a renewed relationship. And he has become our best walking testimonial to restoring relationships in the family.

You will discover that newspapers, radio stations, and other churches are anxious to receive news of family programs. These organizations may be hungry for resource people in the field of family.

You should also cultivate relationships with key community leaders. Talk with school principals and day care directors. Let reporters, not just the religion editor, know that you are available to discuss the family. Once again, creativity and imagination are more powerful than dollars and cents.

Budgeting and Financial Planning

You must be able to handle whatever size budget you have to work with. Expertise in budgeting is vital when the ministry is young and untested. The ability to show positive results for dollars spent can be especially helpful for business-minded church leaders. The problem is, much of the good accomplished by the family ministry is intangible. Occasionally, we will combine a testimonial with the budget presentation to the leaders to put flesh and bones on the helping process.

If the ministry grows to the point that a Christian counseling center is considered, financial expertise is a must. The minister, who now functions as a clinical director, will take on the responsibilities of budgeting, salaries, insurance, fees, and many other fiscal tasks.

Multiple Staff Operations

Many family life ministers will be part of a larger ministerial team. Others will be in the number two position or part of a church planting team. Whatever your position in the orchestra pit, you need to learn how to function in the second chair.

You must be involved with other staff ministers. You should view your role as trainer and equipper of other ministers in the area of marriage and family. Your goal is to train many family life ministers in the staff ranks. Each minister can be equipped with the skills to be a people helper, recognize serious family problems, and integrate the work with the family life ministry.

I believe the seasoned family life minister will become a minister to ministers. The stresses and pressures placed on the local minister and the family are enormous. Someone on-site should be available to help staff marriages and families. The family minister may serve as an advocate to the church leadership for family care, vacations, adequate time off, or other practices that preserve family life in the ministry.

Recruiting, Training, and Maintaining a Volunteer Organization

You will need the people skills to attract highly competent workers, train them adequately, and send them forth with missions meaningful to them. Family ministry is an enormous undertaking in most churches. It demands the involvement of many people in many roles. It also surfaces individuals with unique gifts that have been undiscovered. Your ability to see talent in individuals that has remained untapped will enable you to build a core of enthusiastic volunteers committed to the dreams of family life ministry.

Working with Diverse Populations

Learning to sit by wells implies an ability to learn from the experiences of others. You must be willing and able to enter the experiences of a variety of family forms. You must be able to learn from those families without passing judgment or drawing quick conclusions. Single-parent, blended, and dual-career families are dying for someone to understand their unique struggles.

Working with Church Leaders

You are in the unique position of working for a group of people, educating them beyond their initial understandings of family ministry, challenging their family prejudices, and ministering to their marriages and children. It is a tightrope act at best. But walking this tightrope provides many opportunities to effect change in the lives of church leaders.

What a refreshing sight it is to see a church leader change perspective on the "ideal family"! What a fulfilling moment it is to stand with a deacon or staff minister who abandons denial and walks for the first time down the lonely road of death or divorce! How appropriate it is to hear the leader who was the most resistant to family ministry now espousing the basic principles and proudly carrying the banner! These changes do not come about by accident. They are a part of God's plan working through a ministry to families with a wise leader in service to Him.

Interpersonal Relations, Human and Organizational Relations, and Conflict Resolution

Probably no competency comes closer to describing the daily activities of the family life minister than this one. You are constantly involved with people's lives. You are a coach and trainer of effective communication skills. You must model these skills to other staff members and the church at large. With a background in human systems, you will have a greater understanding of the functioning of the church as a family of families. Finally, you will be called to assist in a wide range of conflict negotiation situations—ranging from issues in the counseling room to issues of vision among church members and leaders.

Goal Setting, Strategic Planning, Implementation, and Evaluation

You help the church choose paths that lead to greater family health. The church must learn to focus on goals for family life ministry that accomplish this.

You should help the leaders of the church focus on reasonable and manageable goals. You should help generate a strategic plan based on those needs, implement the plan, and then evaluate the progress of the ministry.

This is not to imply that an effective family minister is not involved with people. A competent family minister will constantly battle having any time for planning, evaluation, and study because the needs of families are so great.

Training and Practicing Effective Evangelism Through the Family Ministry

Meeting basic human needs is a natural entree into the spiritual lives of families. When people realize the church is concerned about all of their needs, they are more likely to open their hearts to God's Word.

I vividly remember watching a young man approach my family life center one fall morning. He opened the front door and asked my secretary if he might speak with the director. He had heard it was a place where people studied the Bible, and that's what he wanted to do! Our conversations were natural and unstrained. The key to our evangelistic success was the care and concern demonstrated by our family counseling and classes.

Leadership Skills and Developing Leadership Skills in Others

One of my greatest joys in ministry is discovering undeveloped leadership talent. Our churches are overflowing with highly skilled individuals who are capable of tremendous ministries. The family minister's job is to uncover and develop this talent among the men and women in the local church.

You must be a model of effective leadership. You set the pace for the entire ministry. That does not mean you function as an autocratic leader. That does mean you practice listening skills, service, and consistency, and you challenge the church to better living. You can help the church tremendously by living a transparent and authentic life. Your modeling will be more powerful than fifty sermons.

You should function in two roles that, although not competencies, are critical to the life and health of the local church. The first role is that of family advocate. In this role, you speak for the rights and protection of all families in the local church. You offer insights into the feelings of unchurched people as they come to the church.

I have been amazed at the number of decisions made with no regard for the impact on the families of the local church. Schedules are set with no regard to children's sleep needs or parents' work schedules. Ministry demands are made with no regard for competing ministry demands. Members are exhausted, and leaders are frustrated.

You must stand in the breach and articulate the struggles of the contemporary family to the leaders of the church. You must help them understand the pains of a single mother who gets up early, drops off her child at day care, and then rushes downtown to her job. Her evenings are filled with traffic jams, long lines at the express checkout, dinner, housecleaning, and a million other details. Saturdays are not days off, but days to work and fall exhausted into bed. When she and other people like her hear the message, "You are not doing enough, you are not giving enough, you are not committed!" they are rightfully discouraged with the church. You must speak for the voiceless who are slowly ebbing away from the late twentieth-century church.

The second role you must fill is that of a friend to leadership families. In most churches I have been associated with, little attention has been devoted to the care and feeding of leadership families. When crises hit the families, they suffer in silence or resign. You should have your antenna up for the needs of the staff and leadership families under your care.

This is not to say that you become their counselor. You may simply let these people know that you are a safe harbor to come to for consolation, compassion, and referral if needed. The ranks of Christian leadership have been decimated in recent decades because of the lack of family care in the local church.

As a novice family life minister, you will not possess all of these competencies, but you should be working toward mastery of them. The job expectations will change from setting to setting, but a comprehensive family life ministry will call for the skills represented by ministry, marriage and family therapy, and adult education.

Is This for Me?

Perhaps your purpose in reading this book is to clarify your interest in family life ministry. A family minister's job is unlike other traditional staff ministry roles. The job crosses over the barriers of many ministries and age groupings.

The family minister must balance many plates in the air at one time. You should enjoy a work environment that is fast-paced, diverse, and challenging. Some of the more prominent characteristics of the family minister are noted here.

A Lifelong Learner

You must maintain your professional and theological edge by constantly studying. A learning attitude should be an underlying approach to your whole ministry. Families and family ministry will educate you. Families will teach you how to minister to them if you will listen.

Pioneering Spirit

Building a healthy family today runs counterculture. You must enjoy helping cut new paths with families. You must also help the church cross bridges in developing as a faith family.

Independent Initiator

Initiating leadership is essential to the effective management of the family life ministry. If you enjoy initiating and seeing plans developed by others, you will thrive in the family ministry environment.

Focus

The needs of families are so great that many family ministers quickly feel like twenty-four-hour ambulance services. I learned early on to carry a notebook and pen with me at all times. The endless conversations concerning a friend or coworker, a relative or a recommended book filled my Sundays. It is very fulfilling to help, but without focus, the family ministry would never get back upstream to build some dams and prevent family problems from occurring.

Sense of Humor

Family problems are devastating. Spending years walking with people through the valley of the shadow can be very sobering. It is easy to lose a sense of humor or become cynical about human suffering. The ability to turn off the dial, enjoy life, and delight in your family is an essential characteristic.

Tenure

I believe that the best family ministry is accomplished by people who are willing to work with congregations for extended periods of time. Sometimes a move is beyond one's control. Yet, a family minister who is with the church for the long haul will provide a framework for building trust and confidence in the person and the ministry.

Often, the best remedy for barriers to family ministry is the ongoing relationship between the minister and the church. I have seen family ministry carved out of solid rock, and in each case a common denominator in the success of that ministry was the long tenure of the family minister.

Leadership

I mentioned this as a competency, but I list it again here as a personal characteristic. Family ministry needs champions, men and women who are willing to exercise their gifts as church leaders. The church needs credible leaders, people who will not leave the job to an unmotivated committee or garner all the power around themselves and throw out everyone else's creativity. Leadership is a gift that must be cultivated and matured. It is less dependent upon age than upon wisdom. If leadership is your gift, my challenge to you is to exercise it!

Love of People

Family ministry is all about people. We have talked a great deal about goals, needs, and programs. These are all-important so long as you do not lose the perspective of people. If you do not genuinely enjoy the congregation and feel compassion toward them, you are not going to minister effectively.

We read that Jesus viewed the masses and "was moved with compassion for them, because they were weary and scattered, like sheep having no shepherd" (Matt. 9:36). One of the greatest gifts you can help a church cultivate is congregational compassion. To do this, you must be a person of understanding and insight. There is no substitute for people skills in the family ministry business.

Creativity

Family ministry offers new avenues for creativity. Whether it is counseling, teaching, preaching, or program design, you can create and define the ministry with great freedom.

Consider the opportunities current television programs and motion picture productions provide in illustrating family issues. Consider the impact that modern drama can have depicting healthy family patterns to couples who grew up in unhealthy families. The lyrics of many modern songs contain insights into the tragedy of the human experience in sex, drugs, unfulfilling relationships, and self-deception.

The field of family ministry is "white unto harvest" for the inventive mind. Creative individuals will enjoy the work of family ministry and help further define the field for those coming after them.

Ethics and Credibility

Family ministry is no place for the fainthearted. It is not a convenient place to hide out from the world. It is not a work given to replicating the same ministry year after year. As one friend put it, "He has twenty-five years of experience, but it's the first year twenty-five times over!"

The future of modern ministry lies in our ability to answer the credibility questions facing us today. The family minister must walk the tightest line of personal ethics and integrity. Confidentiality and credibility must be unquestioned in the congregation. The minister should be known for a reputation of honesty, responsibility, and truthfulness.

The First Year

What can you expect during the first year of your ministry with a new congregation? Each church is unique, but several trends occur during the break-in period of the new ministry. There is no specific time line for these trends, and many of them occur simultaneously. Some begin almost upon arrival of the new minister; others are initiated when the ministry becomes active.

The Retread Trend

With the availability and popularity of counseling, especially in urban areas, many people are therapy smart. They have long-standing issues, and the list of counselors they have consulted is often long and impressive. They are the counseling retreads. Not particularly interested in changing, they will make an appointment to try out the new family minister. Some even make it a game. They come with wild, exaggerated stories of personal conquests and deeds. This is not therapy; it's their entertainment!

The Core Pain Trend

Many churches, especially highly evangelistic or numerically growth-oriented congregations, have ignored or denied the pain among the people. Suffering people on the outer core of the church tend to exit quickly, forming a portion of the now famous backdoor problem. People in the inner core remain silent and in pain. They will eventually leave, but their departure is often slower and more noticeable.

When the people who are the standard-bearers begin streaming into your office, you know you're working with a growing church that has no concept of edification. Somewhere along the line it neglected the idea that as evangelistic efforts increase, the need for edification goes up. Three thousand were baptized on Pentecost (evangelism), but it wasn't too long until special servants were appointed to meet the needs of neglected widows (edification).

The Definition Trend

Definitions of the family minister and the minister's tasks vary from church to church and from member to member. You should have forged most of these issues in the interview process. The next step is to communicate this understanding to the church. Ideally, this would be done by the leaders, but it may fall upon you to self-define your mission. Members' definitions may range from crisis counselor to youth minister. This defining process is usually not difficult, but it is necessary.

The Counseling Trend

We have defined family ministry as preventive and therapeutic, with an emphasis on the preventive. During the initial phases of family ministry, you may feel inundated with calls for counseling. You may think that you will never be able to move to a more proactive stance because fires are constantly breaking out. In this initial period, you can learn a great deal about the congregation and the community.

This call for counseling will likely continue until you can bring on additional counseling resources. The importance of clarifying your role during the interview process is clear. Without a clear vision for family ministry, the church will have a Christian counselor who teaches some classes.

The Shotgun Trend

The congregation may be so excited to finally have a family life minister that they present you with a cafeteria of demands for time and programs. Requests to visit the school, drop by the office, do a company seminar, speak to the PTA, meet my neighbor, work up these lessons, and recommend a good book will come quickly. You will feel like a shotgun going off—you're putting a lot of shot into the air, but you aren't sure you're hitting anything.

In this phase people will get to know you and feel some ownership in the ministry. After all, you are in the business of activating people to ministry. You will discover some people who will be wonderful assets to the ministry. You will get acquainted with the community. You will also gain valuable insights into the problems confronting the family. This information can be plowed into the needs analysis and ministry plan of action.

The Forgotten Soldiers Trend

Family ministry surfaces some forgotten people. One of my favorite coworkers came to church every Sunday dressed like a reject from a 1967 peace demonstration. He was unique. After the family ministry had been presented to the church, he stopped by to visit with me in the foyer. I was immediately drawn to him because of his quiet wit and sincerity.

I met him that week for a burger and we talked. He told me that he owned the largest chain of heroin addiction clinics in the state. He worked with dozens of therapists and hospitals and hundreds of clients. He wanted to know if I could use a guy like him in my ministry. I was stunned. I asked him how long he had been a member of that church. I discovered that for the past five years he had sat unused and undiscovered in the church pew, three rows from the back. He became one of our most faithful workers.

The family ministry will surface some wonderful forgotten soldiers of the cross, men and women who are anxious to serve in the kingdom of God and just waiting to be discovered. They will quietly approach and softly ask. If you are perceptive, you will find several pearls of great price!

Conclusion

To be a family minister, you must possess a unique blend of talents and training. You are many things to many people. To some, you are a counselor in a crisis; to others, a teacher or resource person. To the community, you are a representative of the church who doesn't talk "that religious jargon." To those in ministry, you are a trusted confidant.

One trait or characteristic supersedes all the others. It is a sense of calling to the ministry of God's family. I can truly say that it is a privilege to minister to marriages and families. The rewards far outweigh the demands made on time and family. The person who will be successful in family ministry will be the person who has a genuine heart for ministry, a heart of compassion for the suffering silent, and an insight into the healing mind of God.

People frequently say to me, "I don't know how you can go through all those messes with people. That would just wear me out!" But isn't that the essence of valid ministry? Isn't it men and women who are willing to roll up their sleeves in the messes of modern American culture and come out with fewer answers and a greater dependence on the grace of almighty God?

Family ministry is for God's faithful plodders, people who are willing to let God faithfully lead them in ministry, people who are willing to lose numerous battles in the fight for the family, yet claim the ultimate victory in Jesus Christ. Godly plodders who view *success* from a heavenly definition, not an earthly one, will find the calling and mission of family ministry the most compelling force experienced in this life. For them, it becomes a reason to be used up in ministry to the Cross.

Competencies are important. Personal characteristics are vital. But a genuine heart of ministry to families is indispensable if you are to survive in family ministry. There is no substitute.

Epilogue

And at this point His disciples came, and they marveled that He talked with a woman; yet no one said, "What do You seek?" or, "Why are You talking with her?"

The woman then left her waterpot, went her way into the city, and said to the men, "Come, see a Man who told me all things that I ever did. Could this be the Christ?" Then they went out of the city and came to Him.

In the meantime His disciples urged Him, saying, "Rabbi, eat."

But He said to them, "I have food to eat of which you do not know."

Therefore the disciples said to one another, "Has anyone brought Him anything to eat?"

Jesus said to them, "My food is to do the will of Him who sent me, and to finish His work. Do you not say, 'There are still four months and then comes the harvest'? Behold, I say to you, lift up your eyes and look at the fields, for they are already white for harvest! And he who reaps receives wages, and gathers fruit for eternal life, that both he who sows and he who reaps may rejoice together. For in this the saying is true: 'One sows and another reaps.' I set you to reap that for which you have not labored; others have labored, and you have entered into their labors" (John 4:27–38).

Who are we as family life ministers in this story? We are not the woman; she is the object of our ministry. We are not the Messiah; He is the model for our ministry. We are not the

Samaritan villagers; they are the dreams of our ministry. We are the disciples.

We are the disciples gone to fetch bread for the Master. While we are gone, history is made! When we return, we do not understand. Do we go reluctantly down the hillside as some of them must have gone? Are our heels dug into the rock as we descend? Do we wonder where the Master is leading us? Or do we willingly walk into the village because we have learned to sit by wells?

I believe the epilogue to the well at Sychar comes three or four years later. After Christ's death, a disciple passed that way again. He stopped and gazed at that well, remembering those amazing two days with Jesus. Then he made a decision. He decided to descend to that little village again or to move on quietly down the road.

You see, we are that disciple standing in the fork of the Samaritan road. All around us are struggling families. And someday when the Master returns, He will ask us, "Did you learn to sit by wells?"

Appendix:

CONGREGATIONAL FAMILY NEEDS ANALYSIS SURVEY FORM

1. What is your sex?

   ____ male   ____ female

2. What is your age?

   ____ 18–25   ____ 35–44   ____ 55–64

   ____ 26–34   ____ 45–54   ____ 65 or over

3. What is the highest level of education you have completed?

   ____ less than 12 years   ____ some college

   ____ high-school graduate   ____ college degree

   ____ technical or   ____ postgraduate work
   business school   ____ graduate degree

4. What is your primary occupation?
   (Check the one that best fits you.)

_____ homemaker _____ self-employed _____ unemployed
_____ skilled trade (carpenter, electrician, technician, foreman, etc.)
_____ semiskilled worker (clerical, sales, delivery, etc.)
_____ professional/management (teacher, doctor, lawyer, accountant, administrator, etc.)

5. About how many hours a week are you employed outside your home?
   _____ 0-5 _____ 6-20 _____ 21-40 _____ 41-55 _____ over 55

6. What is your current marital status?
   _____ married   _____ separated   _____ remarried
   (If one of the following, skip to #9.)
   _____ never married   _____ divorced, not   _____ widowed
                                    remarried

7. How many years have you been married to your present spouse?
   _____ 5 or less _____ 6-10 _____ 11-20 _____ 21-30 _____ over 30

8. How would you rate your overall satisfaction with your marriage?
   _____ very satisfied   _____ somewhat dissatisfied
   _____ somewhat satisfied   _____ very dissatisfied

9. About how many years have you attended this church?
   _____ 2 or less _____ 3-5 _____ 6-10 _____ 11-20 _____ over 20

10. About how often do you attend church services/activities?
    _____ 2 or more times a week   _____ once or twice a month
    _____ once a week   _____ less than once a month

11. Do any of the following family members live in town? (Check all that apply.)

_____ parent(s)   _____ brothers/sisters   _____ adult children
_____ spouse's parent(s)   _____ spouse's brothers/sisters

12. Does any relative other than your parents, spouse, or children live in your home?

_____ yes   _____ no

13. Do you have stepparents?

_____ yes   _____ no

14. Are you a parent?

_____ yes   _____ no (If no, skip to #17.)

15. Do you have any children living at home?

_____ yes   _____ no (If no, skip to #16a.)

16. If you have children living at home, how many are in the following categories? (Complete all that apply).

	NUMBER		
	NATURAL	ADOPTED	STEP
Age 5 or under	_____	_____	_____
Age 6–11	_____	_____	_____
Age 12–14	_____	_____	_____
Age 15–18	_____	_____	_____
Age 19 or over	_____	_____	_____

16a. If you have minor children not living at home, how many are in the following categories? (Complete all that apply.)

	NUMBER		
	NATURAL	ADOPTED	STEP
Age 5 or under	_____	_____	_____
Age 6–11	_____	_____	_____
Age 12–14	_____	_____	_____

Age 15-18 _____   _____   _____
Age 19 or over _____   _____   _____

17. About how often do members of your family have a family time together with some spiritual emphasis (for example, worship, Bible study, family projects and games, special activities, etc.)?

_____ more than once a week _____ about once a week

_____ once or twice a month _____ about 3 or 4 times a year

_____ rarely, if ever

18. The Family Center Committee wants to help enrich your family experiences through seminars, workshops, classes, study opportunities—whatever you need. From the list below, please check all concerns for which you would like us to provide help.

_____ Parenting

_____ Parenting young children

_____ Parenting teenagers

_____ Stepparenting

_____ Single parenting

_____ Parenting children with special needs:
          please describe _____

          _____

_____ Role of husband

_____ Role of wife

_____ Relating to in-laws

_____ Relating to aging parents

_____ Relating to adult children

_____ Grandparenting

_____ Divorce recovery

_____ Finances/money management

_____ Family worship

_____ Leisure/recreation time usage

_____ Interfaith marriages

_____ Non-Christian mate

_____ Leading your child to Christ

_____ Accepting your own sexuality

_____ Sex education

_____ Alcoholism in the home

_____ Drug abuse in the family

_____ Abuse in the family (physical, sexual, emotional, etc.)

_____ Premarital education/mate selection

_____ Marriage adjustment (newlyweds)

_____ Middle marriage years

_____ Empty nest adjustment

_____ Household management for two-career couples

_____ Ministering as a family

_____ Adjusting to death in the family

_____ Leadership training

_____ Estate planning

_____ Coping with recurring or catastrophic illness or accidents
in the family

_____ Selecting wholesome entertainment

_____ Conflict resolution in the home

_____ Establishing adult friendships

_____ Teaching Christian values in the home

_____ What senior adults offer to the church

_____ Midlife adjustments

_____ Adult single living

_____ Coping with the arrest or imprisonment of a family member

_____ Coping with the disappearance of a family member

_____ Other: _____

_____

19. For which of the following services do you or does someone in
your family have a current need? (Check all that apply.)

_____ Ministry to families with members having special needs (physical, learning disability, etc.)

_____ Coping with alcoholism or drug abuse

_____ Treatment of alcohol or drug abuse

_____ Premarital counseling

_____ Marriage/family counseling

_____ Personal counseling

_____ Vocational guidance

_____ Providing food or clothing for needy families

_____ Coping with unemployment

_____ Delivery of hot meals to elderly persons or persons unable to leave the home

_____ Dealing with violence in the home

_____ Counseling/ministry to unwed mothers

_____ Recovering from rape

_____ Telephone check for senior adults living alone

_____ Relating to aging parents

_____ Baby-sitting

_____ Ministry to persons who are unable to leave the home

_____ Daily quiet time

_____ Single adult issues

_____ Reading for sight-impaired people

_____ Sign interpretation

_____ Other: _____

_____

20. If a group meeting, class, workshop, or seminar were offered on the topics you checked in question #18, would you and/or other members of your family attend if your schedule permitted? (Check all that apply.)

_____ during Bible class   _____ Thursday evenings

_____ Sunday afternoons   _____ Friday evenings

_____ Sunday evenings   _____ Saturday mornings

_____ Monday evenings   _____ Saturday evenings
_____ Tuesday evenings   _____ at a weekend retreat
_____ Community enrichment   _____ weekdays
       (Wednesday evenings)

21. Choose your 3 most preferred formats for delivery. (1=first, 2=second, 3=third)

_____ class or series   _____ workshop
_____ group meeting   _____ self-study
_____ lecture   _____ discussion
_____ film/video   _____ retreat
_____ Other: _____
_____

22. Additional comments: _____
_____
_____

Thank you for your cooperation. Your answers will give us an opportunity to meet your family needs in a better way.

Printed by permission of Dr. Royce Money.
Additional Needs Analysis materials are available from
Family Ministry Consultants
4012 Jones Bridge Circle
Atlanta, GA 30092

About the Author

Don W. Hebbard, Ed.D., is the family life minister and executive of a center for Christian counseling for a large suburban Atlanta, Georgia, church. He has worked in family ministry for thirteen years.